Fruitful
Labor
How to Live
to 104
Gracefully,
Gratefully

Also by Monica Lee

The Percussionist's Wife:
A Memoir of Sex, Crime & Betrayal

How to Look Hot & Feel Amazing in Your 40s:
The 21-Day Age-Defying Diet, Exercise
& Everything Makeover Plan

Truth, Dare, Double Dare, Promise or Repeat:
On Finding the Meaning of "Like" in 1982

Church Sweet Home:
A Renovation to Warm the Soul

Fruitful
Labor
How to Live
to 104
Gracefully,
Gratefully

MONICA LEE

BOOKS

FRUITFUL LABOR

Copyright © 2020 by Monica Lee

ISBN 978-0-9861943-4-4 (paperback)

Cover photos by Paula Stern and Monica Lee
Cover design by Monica Lee
Print book interior design by Monica Lee
Mindfulmonica.wordpress.com

For Cheri, Steve, Tim, Kay, Pat,
Paula, Jacob, Jedd, Kinsey, Betsy & Molly

Contents

Family Tree

Use this "descendant tree" like a map to help navigate the family members named in Grandma journals (I used familiar names here, not formal ones).

LAURA (HENRY)

  Son JIM (MAGGIE, 1st), (DIANNA, 2nd)

    Granddaughter CHERI (DANNY)

      Great-grandson SAM (KELLY)

        Great-great-grandson NOAH

        Great-great-granddaughter GRACELYN

        Great-great-grandson ELIJAH

      Great-granddaughter HILARY

      Great-grandson ERIK (FAITH)

        Great-great-granddaughter MATILDA

        Great-great-grandson DRAKE

    Grandson STEVE (HOLLY)

Grandson TIM (SHERRI)
  Great-grandson TAVIS (NICOLE)
    Great-great-granddaughter PAISLEY
  Great-granddaughter LEAH
Son BOB (KAREN)
  Granddaughter MONICA (STEVE, 1st), (TYLER, 2nd)
  Granddaughter KAY (KEITH, 1st), (CHUCK, 2nd)
    Great-grandson DREW
    Great-grandson LOGAN
    Great-grandson BRECK
  Grandson CURTIS
Daughter MARY (DONNIE)
  Grandson PAT (MARIN)
    Great-grandson COOPER
  Granddaughter PAULA (JOSH)
    Great-grandson EMERSON
    Great-granddaughter EVA
    Great-grandson ETHAN
Son WALLY (JEAN)
  Grandson JACOB (AMY, 1st)
    Great-granddaughter GRACE
    Great-granddaughter LUCY
  Grandson JEDD (SARAH)
    Great-grandson FINN
    Great-granddaughter KARLY
  Grandson KIP

Grandson KINSEY
Granddaughter BETSY (ZACH)
    Great-granddaughter KYMREE
    Great-granddaughter TAYA
    Great-grandchild (in utero)
Granddaughter MOLLY (TORREY)
    Great-grandson KIPTYN
    Great-granddaughter HARLOW

Prologue

WHEN GRANDMA MOVED TO a senior living community at the grand age of 99, a box of the journals she kept for two and half decades made their way to me, her second-oldest granddaughter.

She wrote about the weather, her walks, visitors and especially good meals in her journals almost every day from 1985 to 2009; I'm missing a few years, but I assume she was writing her thoughts in those years, too. This means she was recording her retirement years in her 70s, 80s and part of her 90s living in a small house and then a cozy little apartment in a bucolic little town in the middle of Minnesota about fifteen miles from where she was born. Few of the entries are earth-shattering or particularly private which sounds a lot like the personal blog I've kept for ten years, but the sheer volume of her records was impressive.

I believe she designated me as the recipient of this treasure trove of memories because she knew I valued the written word. As an adult, I'd written Grandma at least once a month and especially when I traveled out of the country, an opportunity she never had the chance to take. I liked telling her about different places around the country or the world, and I know she appreciated the mail. A visit would have been even better, but a letter in the mailbox was a close second. She always returned the correspondence.

As I was inventorying the cache of diaries, I looked up a few dates with particular importance to me.

For instance, I found a couple of entries about a visit she paid to me when I was attending St. Cloud State University in St. Cloud, Minnesota. I would have transferred there from another university just two months before. I have no memory of this visit, but then, I was pre-occupied:

> *November 14, 1987: A beautiful day. Went to the church sale and left at 10 with [daughter-in-law and my mother] Karen to go to St. Cloud to see the girls. Got to Monica's at 12:30; had egg sandwiches and cookies and then shopped all p.m. Had supper at Perkin's Restaurant. Monica's boyfriend was also with us.*

This "boyfriend" would have been the man who later became my first husband. We would have been dating for about a month so I'm sure we were moony eyed.

> *November 15, 1987: Another nice morning. Slept very good last night. Went to Monica's church at 10:30, had dinner at McDonald's and then shopped some more. Left for*

home at 3:20. I got home here at 5:30, then I went to [son] Wally's for a while.

Mom and Grandma must have slept at the apartment I shared with my friend Jill, but I have no idea where they would have slept—I don't even remember having a decent couch.

On the occasion of my first wedding, she wrote, "It was a very nice wedding and a very good dinner at Pine Cove" without mentioning either my name or the groom's. It made me laugh. But understand, Grandma wasn't writing these entries for anyone but herself. I can imagine they were helpful in reminding her the last time she visited the eye doctor or how she celebrated someone's birthday the previous year.

Still, there are some insightful bits. Here's what she wrote on September 11, 2001:

> *Just when the van was ready to come, [son] Jim came and told me a high-rise building in New York was hit by two planes. The hijackers were piloting. It spoiled my whole day. I hate war. [Friend] Ruth and I rode the van to Perham. She had an appointment at the clinic, so we didn't get home 'til 2. All on TV was about the terrorists. Makes me nervous. [Sister-in-law] Nancy stopped in."*

Grandma was 86 in 2001, so she'd seen more than her fair share of American conflicts and, more than a lot of people, could make a judgment about war.

Grandma, as you might expect, was not computer savvy, so in order to pinpoint some of the more valuable entries and to ask questions, I created a group on Facebook to share and discuss the entries with my aunts and cousins. I anticipated learning more about Grandma but in an unexpected windfall, I also learned more about the rest of my extended family, which is the ultimate gift of these diaries.

⌘

ONE OF THE BEST birthday cards I received when I turned 43 was from my spunky grandmother, who was 95 by then.

The card was personalized, just for me. The words on the front began with my first name and then, "Know what's nice about a granddaughter like you?"

Printed inside: "Everything! It seems like a perfect time to tell you when I'm thinking about you on your birthday ... hope it's a good one! Best wishes and lots of love from Grandma Laura!"

Obviously, someone gave Grandma a box of personalized cards so that Grandma had a card to remember each of her grandchildren's birthdays. It was a brilliantly useful gift for a woman who had pretty much everything, and it made Grandma look like a star.

The card was customized just for me and arrived right on my birthday, but those weren't even the best parts. Inside, my grandmother who was normally stingy with praise, wrote a note.

Usually, she discussed the weather, who visited recently and her plans for the coming week. She covered that, too, but the card apparently opened the door to some uncharacteristic kudos. Her note began like this:

"This card is right—you never forget about me. While on a trip, I always get cards from you."

Grandma was correct on that long-ago birthday and now, too. I will never forget about her. This book about my grandmother and how she lived to be 104 draws on her diaries, her letters, my memories and the memories of some of the other people in our family and community who will never forget her either.

For to me to live is Christ, and to die is gain.
If I am to live in the flesh, that means fruitful labor for me.
Yet which I shall choose I cannot tell.
I am hard pressed between the two.
My desire is to depart and be with Christ,
for that is far better. But to remain in the flesh
is more necessary on your account.

~ Philippians 1:21-24

ONE

Quilting

THE FIRST OF GRANDMA'S diaries she gifted to me was from 1985. It's a wire-bound book titled *The Quilt Engagement Calendar 1985*. Grandma would have been 69 on January 1 when she began writing. I'm guessing someone gave it to her for Christmas because they knew she liked to quilt. Her second entry confirms this interest:

> *January 2, 1985: Went to [sister] Freda's to help put a quilt up. She is stitching for [her daughter] Virginia's birthday; quilted till 5. [Fellow quilters] Ruth, Phyllis, Charlotte and Nancy were also there in the night. I quilted on a wall hanging I'm making for [granddaughter] Cheri for the great-grandchild that is coming. [Son] Wally stopped for a few minutes; he had been to the store and got milk.*

Grandma was an experienced seamstress who knew her way around a sewing machine and a quilt rack.

"I have many, many memories of growing up in Blowers Township," my aunt Mary remembers. "Quilting parties, birthday parties, Christmas, mom sewing clothes for all the special occasions."

My uncle Wally, grandma's youngest son, remembered a jacket Grandma make for him as a boy. "Wally did not like it and let her know," recalled my aunt Jean, telling his story for him after his death. "Grandma's sister's sister-in-law, I can't recall her name now, really scolded him for being so ungrateful."

Grandma was an accomplished quilter and belonged to a quilt club most of her adult life. One of my earliest memories of her living room included a quilt stretched across the expanse of it where she and her friends were working on it, one tiny stitch at a time. This was not work but fun.

Many days in her diaries, she wrote something about her hobby. "Did a little stitching on the quilt in the p.m. and night." "Went quilting at Clarine's." "The sewing club tied a quilt." "Tonight, I cut quilt blocks."

She made dozens of quilts including at least one for each of her children, grandchildren and most of her great-grandchildren. The gift of a quilt is a handmade wonder that represents a huge commitment of time. I imagine Grandma thinking of the recipient with every stitch, thus a quilt represents emotional weight as much as an investment of time.

Her diaries are a quilt of sorts, too. Each day is its own unique block, yet knitted together, patterns emerge, colors coordinate, one sees how much they have much in common. The resulting tapestry tells its own story.

Two

104 years

Centenarians are rare. According to the 2010 U.S. Census, there were just 53,364 people 100 or older living in the United States. Ten years later, nearly all of them have left this earthly plain. A new, and probably larger group of centenarians has replaced them. In the period 1980 to 2010, the centenarian population experienced a larger percentage increase than did the total population, meaning more Americans than ever are living to this triple-digit age.

I found these and other facts in Centenarians: 2010, a publication of the U.S. Census, and I bothered to look them up in honor of my grandmother, who was one of them when she turned 104 in early 2019.

One-hundred-and-four! Can you imagine? Even she couldn't imagine. She said more than once she didn't know why she had lived so long.

Minnesota was No. 10 among states with the highest number of centenarians as a percentage of the population, at least back in 2010. The states with the most as a percentage of the population? North Dakota was No. 1, South Dakota was No. 2, Iowa was No. 3 and Nebraska was No. 4. Go Midwest! The states with the most in raw numbers? Not surprisingly, it was some of the states with the highest overall populations: California, New York and Florida.

As a white woman who lived four years in an elder-care facility in north Central Minnesota, Grandma typified what a centenarian looked like in the United States; 82.8 percent of centenarians were female, and 82.5 percent were white. Almost unbelievably, about a third of centenarians lived alone in their household; the rest lived with others in the household, in a nursing home or in other group quarters.

To better describe my grandmother, it might help you to know she was a farmer's wife with four children and a host of grandchildren, great-grandchildren and great-great-grandchildren. She had a great sense of humor, was a gracious host and had just enough vanity to have kept herself in good shape for ten and half decades. She was petite and thin her entire life, and I remember her with coarse copper-brown hair, cropped close. She made her home among the rolling hills of Otter Tail County, a county known to be heavily wooded through its center and home to a thousand of Minnesota's 10,000 lakes. The most impressive fact about her may be that she has lived through 104 Minnesota winters; other

Minnesotans impressed with their own toughness might tell you frozen storage is why she lived so long.

Laura Becker was born March 8, 1915, in Minnesota to a man who was born in Hanover, Germany, and a German woman born in Wisconsin. Germans are known world-wide for being hard-working, standoffish and, like the Swede Grandma married, direct.

Grandma was thoroughly German, and interestingly, the world she grew up in was multilingual. German was spoken at home, and she remembered having neighbors who spoke only Finnish. "I never spoke German as my only language but when [my older sister] Freda started school, she spoke German and my parents spoke German," Grandma once told an interviewer. "Freda had quite a time in school, so we all switched over to English."

I myself do not identify myself as Scandinavian or even European. If anything, I identify myself as a former Minnesotan (with a mixed heritage of Minnesotan and North Dakotan). Perhaps at some point in this century American children will create pie charts of their heritage labeled with the names of states rather than countries.

Not only do people identify themselves differently now, the world changed in considerable ways during the century my grandmother lived through:

⌘ Civil War veterans were still alive when my grandmother came into the world as a baby on March 8, 1915.

⌘ Wilbur and Orville Wright made four brief flights at Kitty Hawk, North Carolina, with their first powered aircraft twelve years before my grandmother was born.

⌘ The Model T automobile had been in production seven years in 1915.

⌘ My grandmother was 54 when Neil Armstrong walked on the moon.

⌘ The first computer was invented when Grandma was 31; her second son grew up to work on room-sized computers for Control Data.

⌘ Lund Boats was founded when Grandma was 33; two of her sons eventually worked for the popular fishing boat manufacturer based in New York Mills, Minnesota.

⌘ Ray Kroc founded McDonald's when Grandma was 40, but the town she lived in most of her life was so small it still doesn't have one of these ubiquitous fast food franchises.

⌘ The first Wal-Mart opened in Arkansas when Grandma was 47.

⌘ The world's first television station began when my grandmother was 13; her son (my father) would one day make a living selling and repairing TV sets.

⌘ In her final two decades of life, my grandmother's only source of income was Social Security, which was created by Franklin Roosevelt when my grandmother was 20.

⌘ In her lifetime, there were 91 Academy Awards, 53 Super Bowls, 26 U.S. presidential elections, seven major U.S. wars, and seven losses by the Chicago Cubs in the World Series. The Cubs won once.

The dramatic changes in culture and technology that made over the world only changed her marginally. My cousin Cheri once pointed out that Grandma never owned a microwave oven, for instance. She never liked air conditioning much (yes, Minnesota gets hot enough in summer that at least some residents have air conditioning). Grandma was hearing impaired and thanks to medical advances pioneered in her lifetime, she wore hearing aids for as long as I knew her; she owned a TV early on, and in later years, she enjoyed it with closed-captioning.

In her diaries, she rarely wrote anything emotional or introspective. Mostly, she stuck to the transactional events of her day. But an example of the entry she recorded on her 94th birthday rather typifies what she valued:

> *Happy Birthday to myself. Woke up in plenty of time to go to church; rode with [a friend] Harley. Got home at 9:20 so took a nap as we left for [daughter] Mary's at 12 for my birthday party. Very nice. All three [grand]babies born in '08 were there. ... Big gifts. Was home again at 6:30. Was hyper so couldn't relax but really tired when I went to bed. [Son] Bob called from Hawaii to wish me a happy birthday.*

Not sure what "big gifts" meant, but I'm guessing it was gourmet jams, stationery and postage stamps or something similarly frugal. This birthday celebration sort of encapsulated her formula for life and longevity: Spirituality, lots of sleep including a daily nap, loving family and gratitude.

Farming & gardening

GRANDMA WAS BORN IN the house on the family farm in Central Minnesota, and she carried an appreciation and skill for growing things throughout her life.

The money-making feature of the homestead farm was the cows.

"I think I was only seven when I learned to milk cows," she once told an interviewer. "We would milk out in the yard. I don't remember how we learned. The cows would just stand still there in the yard." She remembers squirting milk into the barn cats' mouths.

The Great Depression began when she was fourteen, and the family's cows helped them get by.

"We had it better than most families in our area because we milked more cows. We always milked a lot of cows, so we had good milk checks," she remembered. "I had a wonderful childhood. We weren't rich, but the cows gave us what we needed. We had enough money to get by."

Grandma claimed she milked cows until the day she married my grandfather, a Swede who made his living by farming. "I was even given a cow as a wedding present. I could pick the cow I wanted. I picked a blue roan. I'm sure she didn't give the most milk, but I liked how she looked so I didn't care."

Amusing to me anyway, Grandma rarely drank milk, and she didn't particularly like ice cream (coconut anything was her favorite dessert).

As you might expect on a family farm in the early 20th century, Grandma had a number of siblings. She had three brothers, including an older brother who died at birth, and two older sisters. Grandpa, who once dated Grandma's oldest sister but "it always ended in a fight," Grandma said, was nine years older than Grandma. They waited to wed until Grandma was 21.

Grandpa's brother Art married Grandma's second oldest sister Freda (got that? two sisters married two brothers), and my grandparents lived on a farm a mile away from his brother and her sister's farm.

My grandparents raised milk cows, sheep, hogs and chickens. They grew hay, corn and grain to feed the cows. And they always had to grow potatoes. My father remembers his father's face and arms would swell up. He farmed all his life but, he learned in retirement, he was allergic to soil. A farmer, allergic to dirt!

"I'm sure your dad could tell you about how hard mom worked to prepare meals when the thrashers came," my aunt Mary told me.

In a letter to me in the '90s, Grandma wrote: "Happy Thanksgiving! Who will be the cook? You're lucky—in my days, you got your turkey alive and had to shop the head off and pick the feathers and pull the guts. Sounds like fun, doesn't it?"

In the '50s, she raised an acre of cucumbers for Gurney's Pickles and used the money to buy the kids' school clothes. Of course, the children—my dad, his sister and brothers—were required to help pick "pickles." Other neighbors had "pickles," too, and they took turns hauling them into town. Grandma was quite successful, taking in $400, which was big money then.

Art was farming when he was struck down by a stroke in the mid-60s before I was born. My dad tells me my uncle and grandfather took over Art's cows and chores for a while until it became apparent Art would never be able to farm again. I remember nothing of a man who must have been strong and effective as a life-long farmer in north central Minnesota except his halting walk and garbled speech. He and his wife, Great Aunt Freda, were frequent guests around our holiday table because of their close relationships with my grandparents. Art lived for nearly twenty years after his stroke. He scared me as a child because I couldn't understand a word he said; I'd like to think I as an adult would be more kind to him. Dad said Art was most articulate when he swore, which he didn't do much before his stroke, probably because he was frustrated with his state.

After my great uncle and great aunt retired, my grandparents retired from farming, too, and moved to the same small town only a few miles from the farms. This meant Grandma lived within twenty miles of her birthplace her entire life.

None of Grandma's children became farmers, and the farm was sold but Grandma kept growing things.

As one who appreciated aesthetics, Grandma always had flowers. "Always had what I call a grandmother's flower garden mix: marigolds, cosmos, bachelor buttons, bells of Ireland, poppies, daisies," one of her daughters-in-law remembered.

"Whenever I see bells of Ireland, I think of Aunt Laura," Grandma's niece Diane remembered. Grandma also had a knack at keeping Christmas poinsettias alive long after Easter, sometimes even years later.

A remembered inventory of Grandma's flowers was never complete without her fern peonies. "Grandma inherited them from (her sister) Emelia," Dad said. "All the kids inherited them. Very expensive at the green house."

She also had apple trees in back yard. An apple a day, you know, keeps the doctor away.

Her yard was as big as half a football field, and at 88, she still used a push mower to cut the grass. Her sons would promise to mow it for her, but she would become impatient and fire up the mower herself.

And she always grew long sweet grass. "It needed to be burned in spring. Grandma used to burn it," my father remembers, "but (her son) Wally dreaded doing it. It would just blow up in flames."

A lifetime of gardening was not abandoned when she moved from her house to an apartment that relieved her of yard work. Even at 99, she grew tomatoes, lettuce and radishes on her back porch.

Her farmer's wife perspective carried through her life. When she was 102 and living at in the elder care center, she told my aunt Mary: "Must have been a good year for farmers. I know the men had good seed this year as every woman that works here is pregnant."

FOUR

A wife, a widow

GRANDMA GOT MARRIED WHEN she was 21. Henry, the jovial Swede she married, was nine years older than she.

"My husband had a great personality," she once told an interviewer. "He always talked to everybody. He was charming and loved kids. He always said he had to wait to get married because he had to wait for me to grow up."

Laura and Henry had, by all accounts, a happy and productive marriage for forty-one years until Henry died of emphysema.

Grandma never remarried.

She remembered her beloved husband often in her diaries, frequently on symbolic days.

> *June 6, 1986: Fifty years ago today, I became the wife of Henry Wallgren but now I've been alone for eight years.*

> *October 23, 1986: It was 9 years ago that Henry died today.*

Grandma Laura and Grandpa Henry

October 23, 1987: *10 years ago, Henry died and 9 years ago Leroy [a nephew].*

October 23, 1988: *It was 11 years ago today that Henry died.*

February 18, 1989: *Today would have been Henry's birthday. [Eldest son] Jim's [family] and I got flowers to put on altar for Henry's birthday.*

October 23, 1990: *It was 13 years ago today Henry died.*

October 23, 1991: It was 14 years ago since Henry passed away.

October 23, 1993: 16 years ago that Henry died.

February 18, 1995: Would have been Henry's birthday today he would have been 89.

October 23, 1995: It's 18 years ago since Henry died.

June 6, 1997: [Sister] Freda treated me to breakfast for my 61 years of being married.

October 23, 1998: Twenty-one years ago today, that Henry passed away. I hoped at that time I wouldn't live to be 80 and now I'm 83. Have had good years, too.

October 23, 2002: 25 years ago today, Henry died. Weather was beautiful at that time, and we've had it so cold now.

June 6, 2004: 68 years ago, I became the bride of Henry. '36 was a hot and dry year; it was a beautiful morning today.

October 23, 2006: It's 29 years ago that Henry died.

June 6, 2007: Was very nostalgic here all day; was our 71st wedding anniversary today.

October 23, 2007: 31 years ago, Henry died.

She's wistful in these entries, but not particularly effusive. Grandma's emotions were like that; she had them, but they were generally concealed, probably a trait of rigidity she cultivated from her German heritage.

Grandma was 100 percent German, and Grandpa was 100 percent Swedish so they shared a character trait of being sometimes uncomfortably direct (ah, so my inability to navigate delicate diplomatic matters can be traced to my heritage).

Grandma liked Lutheran coffee. That's what I call coffee weak enough you can see the bottom of the cup. But when my grandfather was alive, he'd make coffee so strong a spoon could stand up in it.

They might have had differences of opinion on minor subjects like coffee, but they shared important things, like lifestyle and values.

Alvina, Grandma's cousin, shared this memory of the couple. "My brother Ralph mentioned that Henry once gave Laura a black eye," Alvina said. "Of course, it sounds bad, but back then when people slept in much smaller beds, it was more hazardous. When Henry turned over in bed, his elbow caught Laura right in the eye. It made an interesting story back then."

The couple farmed together for decades, and then when my grandparents moved to town, they became janitors at the church.

Grandma earned extra money babysitting and when Grandpa was alive, he helped. (In fact, one of my earliest memories of

Grandma was when she babysat me, my sister and brother overnight. I couldn't sleep, and she made me warm milk with honey. Feeding people was one of the ways she showed her love.)

Laura and Henry raised four children who grew up to live within sixty miles of her. Until she moved to an elder care facility in a nearby town, two of her sons lived in the same town as her; one or the other or both would visit her nearly every day. All of her grandchildren except two lived in Minnesota. Of the two who escaped the buttoned-up boundaries of the state, one lives in a town just across the border in North Dakota, and I am the other one living out-of-state (in Wisconsin).

⌘

MY GRANDPARENTS WERE MARRIED forty-one years before my grandfather died, and in the end, she was a widow longer than she was a wife.

All evidence in Grandma's diaries indicates she never wanted to remarry or even considered it. After Grandpa died, she remade her life in her sweet little Central Minnesota town in a way that made her happy uncoupled. "Laura said she always felt safer living in town because she knew her cousin Walter Windels was on duty patrolling the town," her cousin Alvina said. "It gave her peace of mind after losing Henry."

I'm not an avid football fan, but even I know Joe Namath was one of the greatest quarterbacks of all time.

Out on the PR trail for his memoir *All the Way: My Life in Four Quarters,* Namath was interviewed on National Public Radio. Among other subjects, he talked about aging.

"I decided to make a plan at fifty," he said. "Fifty was halftime, man. And you've seen—I've seen a lot of games won and lost in the third and fourth quarter. I don't want to go out on a bad note. I want to keep growing, being productive, keep learning and keep loving, man. I want to be a positive dude the rest of the way."

Keep growing, keep learning and keep loving. What a great mantra for one's third and fourth quarters.

Grandma's half-time was at fifty-two. Her husband died in her third quarter. But she kept growing, kept being productive, kept learning and kept loving in her second half.

With a grandmother who lived to 104 and me in the midst of my fifty-third year, I could argue I'm just beginning my third quarter, too. I feel like Namath's interview was like a coach's half-time pep talk: Keep growing, keep learning and keep loving, man (woman!). Be a positive lady the rest of the way.

Ooh-rah!

FIVE

Frugality

ONE OF THE MARKERS of a Minnesota native is her spending. Or lack thereof.

There are two kinds of people in the world: The kind who brag about how much they spent on something and the kind like me, with my Minnesota roots and Scandinavian heritage, who tell you about the great deal they scored. It's common to compliment a Minnesota woman on her becoming frock and hear about the size of its discount on the clearance rack.

Grandma subsisted on a Social Security check racked up by a farmer and her babysitting money the entire time she kept her diaries. If ever there were a good argument for keeping Social Security solvent, it's hundred-year-old widows.

Having been a teenager when the Great Depression hit America, Grandma knew well the value of a dollar.

> *October 22, 2004: Stopped at Fleet, bought the boys Christmas gifts. Next stop was Wal-Mart. Really got for everyone else. Then had lunch at Brass Lantern. Then we*

went to $1 store, I couldn't believe what one could get for $1 so the shopping was really easy.

Grandma was never one to be wasteful. All those vegetables she grew in her garden? She ate them. She gave some away. And what she couldn't eat or give away, she stored up for winter. Canning and freezing one's harvest is a great way to save money on groceries. Here's a taste from 1996 of what her autumn diaries read like in many years.

Aug. 1: *Picked pickles and canned them in a.m. In p.m., I mowed a little, picked peas and froze them.*

Aug. 5: *I planned to get up early to pick peas and beans before Clarine came but I overslept till 7:20 so I really had to rush. They were really nice. ... I froze peas and beans tonight.*

Aug. 8: *Went to garden as soon as I got up to pick vegetables, so I froze peas and beans, canned pickles and made two batches of cookies. Was very tired when bed came.*

Aug. 12: *I picked peas and beans as soon as I got up.*

Aug. 13: *Washed and canned pickles and mowed some lawn before noon.*

Aug. 16: *Worked in garden for an hour. Also, pulled the onions.*

Aug. 23: Pulled the peas and beans early this morning and basted binding on a quilt I stitched last year. In the p.m., I went to [senior] center for fruit bingo. I took a pear and came home with grapes.

Her diaries make frequent mentions to fruit bingo and penny bingo, games played at the senior center.

Aug. 26: Picked pickles for Freda as soon as I got up. Had a good picking.

Aug. 27: Canned tomatoes in the morning.

Aug. 31: Phyllis picked me up for coffee and when I got home, I froze corn Jim had gotten.

Sept. 6: Met Freda and Clarine for coffee at Eagles. Freda treated Clarine, and in p.m. I went to fruit bingo. I got a piece of watermelon. Real good. Canned crate of pears and tomatoes when I got home. Was tired when I went to bed.

Sept. 9: Picked tomatoes before Clarine came.

Sept. 10: Picked half the potatoes this morning.

Sept. 15: The weather was beautiful. Mary and Paula picked potatoes, Jedd and Kinsey tilled the garden, Wally mowed, and Donnie put storms on dining room window so I got a lot done.

Sept. 19: *Canned 6^1/$_2$ quarts of tomatoes in the morning.*

Oct. 1: *When I got home, I made apple jelly and cut tomatoes for preserves tomorrow.*

Oct. 2: *Started with my tomato preserves as soon as I got up. Was done at 10.*

⌘

ONE OF THE STORIES of Grandma's good money management is legend in the family. Here's how my dad tells it:

"Around August 1999, a hailstorm went through Mills [that's how the locals refer to New York Mills]. Grandma heard some other residents were getting insurance money for damage to their roofs, so Grandma called me up and asked me to look at her shingle damage in hopes of collecting insurance. [My dad, you may recall, sold televisions for a living and spent a lot of time on people's roofs installing antennas.] But Grandma's shingles were thirty years old.

"I drove over there in my service van. Yup, the shingles were shot, but I couldn't see hail damage. I told her she was out of luck.

"But she didn't take my no for an answer. She tracked down the insurance guy herself. A few days later, he looked at her shingles and said they needed to replace them and paint two sides of the house. He threw in $150 for damage clean-up. The insurance company wanted to settle for $6,000.

"'Take it and run!' I said, thinking us boys could do the work [Grandma had three sons at the time and a half dozen male grandchildren old enough to shingle a roof]. I talked to the insurance guy, and he insisted the work had to be done to his specifications, meaning, by a professional. We got his list of rules, bought the shingles for $3,500, and shingled her "hail damaged" roof in a weekend. We passed the insurance guy's inspection.

"Mom got a new roof and pocketed $2,000 because her boys did it. That was all on her own."

Six

Faith

MORE THAN HER DEVOTION to farming or her love of family or her frugality, Grandma was faithful. An ardent Christian, she believed with a capital B. Her week revolved around going to worship services until she moved into elder care two weeks before she turned 100. Many of my childhood memories of Grandma revolve around the most popular holidays celebrated by Christians: Easter and Christmas.

Grandma was confirmed into the Lutheran church when she was 11, and she attended church regularly until she was 98 when she started using a walker. When she was growing up, she went to church only about once a month in the winter; the weather prevented it from occurring every Sunday.

"I grew up in a good Christian home," she once told an interviewer. "We always said grace before we ate and prayers when we knelt beside the bed—which I still do. I also raised my children in a good Christian home."

When her sister Freda died, she was found kneeling beside her bed, her hands in the prayer position.

It wasn't until my sister married her second husband on a mountaintop in Arizona that any of Grandma's grandchildren dared to be married anywhere other than a church. Here's how she remembered my cousin Tim's wedding:

> *Oct. 26, 1986: Tim's wedding day. Mary and Donnie were here so I made a big breakfast. Wally was here before we got up. Had an early dinner as Cheri was to be at the church early to pin flowers for Tim's wedding so I went later with Donnie. Was a very nice wedding. I even went to the dance: all new-time music. Bob and Karen stopped for coffee after the dance.*

During her early retirement, she was an active member of church volunteer groups, referred to in Midwestern parlance as *Ladies Aid*. These volunteers made desserts for gatherings, arranged flowers on the altar for services, and prepared and cleaned up serving ware and glasses for Holy Communion. High holidays at church called for extra service, which Grandma frequently volunteered to perform.

Christmas Eve at Grandma's was chaos. Imagine a dozen adults and at least two dozen kids high on Christmastime sugary treats packed into her little house or, after she moved, into her little apartment. Everyone brought a dish to pass ("hotdish" in Minnesota parlance), and she provided the turkey or ham. No spread was complete without pickled beets, adored by some, abhorred by others. Half of those in attendance, including Grandma, were hearing impaired, so the decibel level climbed until the whole house reverberated at a low rumble. You could probably hear the Wallgren clan celebrating a block away.

Here's how she described Christmas Eve through the years in her diaries:

1985: *Was very cold this morning. I was busy all morning. Mary's family got here at 11. She had chicken soup. We went to 2 o'clock church. It was very nice. Did a lot of singing. Bob's and Cheri's [families] came as soon as we got home but Jim and Freda and Virginia were late as they were to 4 o'clock services. Had 27 for supper but everything went fine. Mary and Donnie helped clean up and we got to bed at midnight.*

1988: *Esther and I went to church at 9 to arrange poinsettias. We had 19. Mary and family came at 11. We went to 2 o'clock church and the family were all here for supper except Bob's family. There are 22. Freda was also here. I got to many nice gifts.*

1990: *Mary got sick during the night, so she surely didn't feel good. I went to work on altar at 10. Donnie cut the meat while I was gone. We went to 2 o'clock services, picked up Freda, had a very good potluck supper. I asked Carl and*

Ruth, too. Even Santa came which really added a lot. A very cold night.

1991: Today will be busy. All will be here except Bob's two girls [that would be my sister and me; I was living in Ohio in the early '90s]. Mary's family came at 2. We went to the 4 o'clock services. Had candles and a good crowd. Didn't eat 'til 7 as Bob's family had services at 6. Was a lot of excitement when we opened gifts. I had so many nice gifts. Mary and Donnie helped clean up. Weather was very nice.

1992: Not too busy. Just getting things organized for tonight. Mary and Donnie came at noon; had hotdish and sandwiches. Mary's family and I went to 2 o'clock services. Bob's, Wally's and Jim's families all went to 4 o'clock, also Freda. All came here after for a potluck supper. Things were different with [daughter-in-law] Maggie missing [Jim's wife died of cancer in 1992]. When Bob's left to go home, their car wouldn't start so jumped it but didn't work right so they turned around and came back so I made beds on the floor for [grandsons] Curtis and Patrick. Also drank tea before going to bed and very stormy and cold night. Got so many nice gifts, a big assortment of coffee and tea, all different flavors.

1993: Very cold. Jim and Wally and kids stopped in the morning and at 1:30, Mary's family came. We cooked and mashed potatoes and put in slow cooker before we went to church at 4. Had a full church and the family all came from church except Monica and Kay. Had about 28. A nice, happy evening. Got such nice gifts.

1994: *I was very busy this morning. Mary came at noon. We had vegetable soup and sauce, and at 4 we went to candlelight services. They started coming here after that for potluck supper. All were here but Monica and Steve and Kay and Keith. The little kids were really wild before we opened gifts. The weather was 36 degrees at 7.*

1995: *I've been busy. Made a hotdish for our dinner. When Mary got here, they went to Jim's for a little while. Donnie cut the turkey first. We walked to church for candlelight services at 4 and everyone was here soon after we got home again. Monica and Kay weren't here so we were 30. It was nice and weather was beautiful. Wally's brought homemade ice cream for a later lunch.*

1996: *Got to work as soon as I got up. Mary's family came at noon; had chili. Went to 4 o'clock services, candlelight, very nice. Everyone was here as soon as we got home, all but Monica and Steve. Bob's were going there for Christmas. The weather was bitter cold. Got so many nice gifts, and I give so little.*

1997: So much to do when I got up. Went to Donna's at 8:30 for a hair set. Really got busy when I got home. Mary's family came at 12:30 so we got it all done. Went to 4:30 services. Church was overflowing. All came here after. Was a very nice evening. Monica, Steve, Kay and Curtis were missing, also Cheri as she was sick. Weather was beautiful. I went to bed at midnight.

1999: Was busy all morning getting things organized for the family. Mary, Donnie and Paula came at noon. Had split pea soup. The whole family went to 4 o'clock services at 4; had candles. Had supper at 6. Was a very nice evening. Jim's family left early. Then we had Wally's homemade ice cream. Was very tired when I went to bed.

2000: Went to early church but didn't stay for Bible study. Mary's family got here early made corn chowder for noon lunch. Steve stopped with a beautiful flower arrangement. Went to 4 o'clock services. Church was full. Pastor Haakana said he was nervous; he had never spoken to such a big crowd. We left after church for Bob's. Their new house is very nice, and we had plenty of room. Had a very good supper, and I got so many big gifts.

2001: Went to Donna's at 8 for hair appointment. Mary and Donnie got here at 11. I made corn chowder for dinner. Paula was also here. The rest came after 4 o'clock services except *Bob's; they went to Kay's and Chuck's. The weather was cold but not stormy. Church was full. Everyone brought such good food. I didn't feel too good but ate. Pat and Marin came late but went home again as they were expecting company. I felt good again.*

2002: *The big day has arrived. We all went to church at 4. Church was overflowing. Came back here for supper. Thirty-three, but it worked fine, lot of good food. Wally's brought Emelia's big table; I used her big tablecloth; 12 sat at that table. Everyone enjoyed being together. Mary and Donnie stayed overnight.*

2004: *I slept very good. Walked the hallways, and then buttered three loaves of flatbread and did other things getting ready for tonight when the family will come, all but Bob's girls. Thirty and thirty-one with [great-granddaughter] Grace. She was so sweet sleeping most of the night. Everyone wanted to hold her. The food was so good. I took a plate to Mae Johnson's; she was alone. Her husband went to Japan for three months. Ended the night with homemade ice cream Wally brought. We went to the 3 o'clock services; the church was full.*

2006: *Was up but didn't plan to go to 9 o'clock church so did other things getting ready for tonight. Wally and Jedd came and brought the big table in, and three chairs. Jim* *stopped in while they were there getting things ready. I was taking a nap at 1:30 when Mary and Donnie stopped so then I got busy. Soon, Paula, Josh and Emerson came and then Patrick and Marin in a beautiful old Lincoln given to her by her grandparents—a beautiful car. We all went to 3 o'clock services. Church was more than full, and the rest is history. Some were late but all in all it was a wonderful night. I got way too many gifts. So much in good order. Went to bed tired but slept well.*

⌘

SINCE EASTER MORNING ALWAYS began with a sunrise church service, her daughter Mary and family often arrived the day before in order to attend services with Grandma. Eventually, all of Grandma's children and grandchildren would make their way to Grandma's house for a potluck and an afternoon Easter egg hunt. The highlight of the Easter egg hunt at Grandma's house through the years was finding the Golden Egg, a hard-boiled egg Grandma painted gold.

Here's how she described Easter through the years in her diaries:

> *April 19, 1987: We all went to early church and breakfast. Donnie fried the chicken and sliced the ham when we got home. I got to go back to church to take care of communion.*

They had dinner ready when I got back. Everyone but Monica was here.

March 26, 1989: *Kids were up early. We left for church at 7 for rolls and coffee. Really got busy when we got home as we were having potluck dinner here. Jeannie and Betsy didn't feel good so didn't come. Kids had a great time. Everyone left early as some had other places to go. Was also a nice day but very foggy when I went to bed.*

April 15, 1990: *We went to the 8:15 services. It was a full house. Got ready for our potluck dinner when we got home. Had 18 for dinner. Freda was also here. Kids enjoyed their hunt. Had it outside; was it ever cold.*

March 31, 1991: *When I work up, Freda was already up and ready for church. We went to the sunrise services so walked over. It was very nice. Eighteen Easter lilies on the altar and two other plants from Colorful Seasons [the nursery operated by Grandma's grandson Steve and his wife Holly]. Had breakfast at church. Had a very good crowd. Bob's came for the 8:15 services. The family was all here except Mary; she called. The kids enjoyed the Easter hunt. The weather was nice and bright but cool. Had over 700 at the three services.*

For reference, the 1990 census counted 943 residents in New York Mills, a village at least three churches call home.]

April 19, 1992: Got up at 5:30 for sunrise services. Also had breakfast at church. Took a nap again at 9:30. They all came for potluck at noon. Donnie and Jedd were sick so didn't come. Jeannie and Molly stayed with Jedd, but they came in p.m. for the annual Easter hunt. Karen, Freda and I walked to church to get Easter lilies. Also showed the centennial quilts to Karen; very nice. I was very tired in the night but have everything in order before I went to bed. The sun came out and it was beautiful, very warm. Wally was leaving for Chicago at 6.

April 11, 1993: I didn't go to 6 o'clock services but went to 8:15 and had pancakes after. It had snowed during the night, so I wore my boots. It snowed lightly till nearly noon. They all came for potluck dinner except Mary and Freda. Jim brought the ham. We had to have the hunt inside. They had fun. I was tired in the night.

April 3, 1994: Mary and Donnie were up before I was. Went to 8:15 services, also had rolls and coffee. Had 23 for potluck dinner. Monica was happy to be with us again. They all left quite early. Kids were happy over the Easter hunt. We hid outside.

April 16, 1995: I woke up at 5:15. I was happy so I could go to 6 o'clock services. Also had breakfast at church and then I went to 8:15 services. It was early when some came. Bob had a lot of pictures to show of their trip to Missouri. Had 25 here. Mary's family and Kay and Keith didn't come. Had a very nice day. Hid inside for three little ones and the rest outside. Betsy found the Golden Egg. A dark and cold day.

April 7, 1996: To my surprise, I woke up in time to go to the 6 o'clock services. It was beautiful. The Rev. Esala was the speaker. Had rolls, juice and coffee before I came home. Mary and Donnie came early. Had potluck dinner. Very good. We had 25. Had the hunt inside. Kinsey found the Golden Egg. The weather was cool. The three little girls [Grandma's youngest granddaughters and first great-granddaughter] all had long dresses on.

March 30, 1997: I woke up on time to go to 6 o'clock services. Had rolls and coffee after. Had the annual Easter here. I made shipwreck [see Chapter 7 for description of this recipe] and ham. Just Wally's family and Bob's family were here but had a nice time. I still got a birthday gift from Monica and Steve—different coffees, and at 6 I walked to Jim's to see the twins [Jim's second wife Dianna's grandchildren]. They surely are nice babies.

April 12, 1998: I woke up in time to go to the 6 o'clock services. Was a good crowd. Had rolls and juice after. Karen Dreyer made the rolls—good. Had 22 for dinner. Was just Jim's, Tim and Steve missing. Had ham and turkey. Kinsey found the Golden Egg. Weather was sunny but very windy.

April 23, 2000: I got up at 5 to go to sunrise services at 6. Had rolls, coffee and juice after. Dinner isn't too big of a deal—just Bob's, Monica and Steve and Wally, Amy and Drew. Bob's brought ham and potatoes. I had hunt with the girls, and he found the egg with $1. Weather was perfect. Nancy came in the night; said Lillian broke her leg Saturday.

March 31, 2002: Easter and cool cloudy day. Snowed a bit last night. I wore my boots to church as I went to 6 o'clock. Had rolls and coffee. After I came home, they played the new pipe organ and the bells played at the second services. Had a very big crowd. Mary's family came at 11 but was later before Bob's family came. Met [granddaughter] Paula's new boyfriend, too.

April 11, 2004: I woke up at 5:15 so I knew I would be on time for 6:00 services. When I was going to garage, Eunice stopped and offered me a ride, so I went with her. Had rolls and coffee after. I took a nap when I got home. Bob picked me up at 10 and we left to go to Kay and Chuck's. They were still at church, but we went in. Monica and Steve came, too, *had a nice time. The baby [Grandma's great-grandson Logan] had grown. On the way home, we went to St. Cloud to look at house Monica and Steve bought; very nice and very good day.*

⌘

IN 1989, A FIRE gutted the sanctuary of Trinity Lutheran Church, the church Grandma attended when she moved into town.

> **December 9, 1989:** *Freda called me at 11:20 p.m. and told me Trinity church was on fire. I drove to the hall but couldn't see much, just the fire trucks flocking.*

The next day, a Sunday, she noted "the fire did a lot of damage" and services were held at the school.

A week later, she wrote:

> **December 17, 1989:** *Jim picked me up at 8 and we went to the school to set up for church and communion and at 9:30, I picked Freda up and we went to church. Julie came home with me and washed the communionware. Then we went to look at the burnt church. It is so sad to look at.*

At Palm Sunday the following year, the congregation dedicated the new church, which was built across the street from Grandma's house. She could now walk to church.

In a letter to me, she wrote, "Well, we finally had services in our new church. It was beautiful and exciting. [This is perhaps as much emotion to which she ever admitted in writing.] Had 505 people which made it full. We only had one service that day, and visitors, too. Jim has really been excited over it. He furnished the cake for after the service. Cost him $140 but it was nice. Looks like the church now. We are battling mud there. Valerie's wedding is May 5 in the new church. I'm one of the cake cutters. How exciting!"

Her family would someday gather at that church for her funeral.

SEVEN

Hospitality

NOT LONG AGO, I overheard a woman in 30s say she had never made pie.

Never made pie? Kids nowadays *eat* pie but don't *make* it? "Buy pre-made crust," I suggested.

Elaborate desserts like pie and multi-layered cakes might someday be as rare as black bread and figgy pudding, bygone staples of the Renaissance. Which made Grandma part of a dying breed. She made delicious pies, and she sure didn't buy the crust. She made it from scratch.

My mother often marveled at the quality of Grandma's pie crust, but try as she might, Mom couldn't get Grandma to share the recipe.

"Her instructions were 'until it feels right' or 'when it looks like that,'" Mom said.

Dad believed one of her secrets was that she used home-rendered lard and mixed it by hand when she made pies. Home-rendered lard, essentially melted pork fat, was softer and soupier, not so silly and hard as purchased lard, and its use resulted in thin-pie crust. Talk about a tactic employed in a bygone era.

> *July 10, 1998: Went to the senior center at 9 to bake pies. It was just Mary, Ruth and me; Delores supervised. Made 20 pies to take to Phillip Mills tomorrow. It went well. Got home at 11:30.*

Grandma made a pecan pie for my father's 67th birthday. She was 95 at the time. Imagine that: A 67-year-old man celebrated his birthday with a pecan pie made his 95-year-old mother. Minnesota's longevity is all that fresh air and fresh water (land of 10,000 lakes, you know) and hard work, inspired by that German-Scandinavian work ethic. Add generous helpings of pecan pie, and you're not only living longer, you're enjoying it, too. (He shared, and it was delicious!)

Pie wasn't Grandma's only wow effect as she was the gracious hostess.

She loved entertaining and she served "coffee" to her visitors; coffee meant the caffeinated beverage and an array of sandwiches and desserts (in Minnesota, and perhaps elsewhere, a *coffee* is an event as much as a beverage).

For my grandmother, a plate was a stage. A meal was not complete without an elegant backdrop (usually china), a star and supporting players: pickles, pickled beets, a sliced orange or something else tart or colorful. For a savory dish, buttered bread, cookies or pretty garnishes. My grandmother's meals were as much a treat for the eyes as for the stomach.

An elegant coffee, Grandma style.

Realize, of course, visits to my grandmother's house were usually for special occasions or holidays, though I suspect she, like me, used real dishes for her snacks and arranged her food on the plate in a pleasing way; she wasn't the type of person to eat out of the potato chip bag or slop a glob of food on a divided Melmac tray.

Even at 96, she lived on her own and hosted elegant coffees. I remember one visit when she treated me to coffee cake.

But not just any coffee cake.

She made the coffee cake herself that morning. After arguing about the size of piece in which I should indulge (she was ready to serve me twice as much), she prepared the cake to serve. First, my 96-year-old grandmother apologized for not using real whipped cream (that's OK, Grandma) and dolloped a generous portion of whipped topping on the cake. Then she added a pretty spoonful of apple preserves. At that point, I was ready to bring our plates to the table. But no, these plates weren't finished yet.

She retrieved a fresh orange from the refrigerator, sliced off a couple of slices and arranged the pretty orange slices alongside the cake.

Voilà, ready to enjoy.

⌘

Sauerkraut Poem

The sauerkraut commenced to smell,
They can smell no smellier.
We put them in a little barrel,
That's way down in the cellar.
We put them in the barrel,
And we stomped them with our feet.
We stomped them, we stomped them,
And made them nice and sweet.

⌘

EVER EATEN SHIPWRECK? WELL, depending on your perspective, you haven't missed anything. Or, you've missed a really delish dish.

I hate shipwreck. It's one of my father's favorite meals, and I remember pushing it around on my plate wishing for something else when I was in junior high school. There's a reason "wreck" is part of the name.

While visiting my 94-year-old grandmother once, she mentioned she made shipwreck for one of her guests. I made a face, and my stepchildren (who love things like macaroni goulash and tater tot hotdish) asked, "What is shipwreck?"

Well, Grandma said, you start with a layer of onions in a pan, and then you add a layer of potatoes, and then you add a layer of cooked hamburger with a cup of rice in it. Then there's a layer of cooked celery, she continued, and then you add a layer of beans or whatever vegetable you have—"I like corn," she noted—and then you pour white sauce over the whole thing, and you bake it for a long time over low heat. I think that's what makes it good, cooking it a long time, she said.

As she was describing it, I shuddered, but everyone else around the table—my husband, my 20-year-old stepdaughter and my picky 15-year-old stepson—nodded their head like it sounded like the most delicious hotdish ever. I just listened while nibbling on Christmas cookies.

But I don't make it very often, Grandma said, because you have to dirty so many pans before you're all done.

Not believing anyone could like that "wreck" of a dish as much as my dad, I asked my family later, "Did that *really* sound good to you?"

Sure! they replied in unison, why don't you make that?

I don't make hotdishes, especially not a hotdish I won't eat.

But they got the recipe straight from the lips of the ship's captain. If they ever want to eat it, they can make it themselves.

And I'll clean up all the pans in the ship's mess.

⌘

NOTE TO SELF: NEVER quit learning.

I enjoyed the company of my 96-year-old grandmother at an Easter celebration in 2011. She no longer drove, but she still lived on her own in her apartment.

Grandma's Easter cake

As is tradition in our family, guests always offered to bring a dish to a meal, and Grandma agreed to bring a dessert to my parents' house where eleven of us were celebrating Easter. She wasn't up to making pie; bear in mind. So she offered to make a pineapple-strawberry cake, the recipe for which she found in a newspaper, because it looked easier.

Since I hung around with a lot of 40-year-olds at the time who didn't read cookbooks, let alone newspapers, and who thought cookies are a lot more work than pan bars, I was impressed a 96-year-old would be willing to try a new recipe like one for an elegant three-layer cake with pineapple custard frosting and fresh strawberries as garnish.

It was as delicious as it is beautiful. I thanked Grandma for the cake. The life lesson was the icing on top.

⌘

WHEN GRANDMA MOVED FROM her apartment to her new home in a senior living community, she had quite a lot of stuff to shed.

Grandma was about to turn 100. A lifetime of household items still contained in her apartment was distributed among her four children. Thanks to Dad's keen eye and frugal nature, a set of flatware and a collection of her china were among the pieces passed along to me. Dad rescued the flatware literally from the garbage.

Maybe some folks wouldn't be so pleased to inherit china, but I couldn't have been more tickled. Grandma's new china coordinated with and expanded my own collection beautifully.

The plate with the flowery pattern came from from my original china collection, which I acquired upon my first marriage: Vintage Floral Splendor by Johann Haviland. All the other pieces featuring platinum striping (really! platinum!) were Grandma's: Nora by Harmony House.

The Nora plates were just slightly larger and flatter than my Floral Splendor pieces so they made great charger plates or, when I am serving a crowd, they mix-and-match much better than my functional-but-not-very-elegant Longaberger pottery. Grandma's collection includes a gravy boat (oh, joy! to serve gravy properly in a pretty boat instead of a mixing bowl with a spout) and a couple of other serving pieces that are a treat to use at holiday dinners we host.

I distinctly remember eating off of Grandma's china when I was growing up in the '70s and '80s. Grandma was a hostess bar none who appreciated a tasty side dish and a beautiful garnish. I can see in my mind that little saucer filled with a canned peach and cottage cheese, and there was always a spoonful of sweet pickles or pickled beets to accompany the ham or turkey.

Coffee with Grandma was always an occasion. It was never just coffee. At the very least, there would some sort of cake or pie and cookies (cookies were always accents, not the main dish), but usually it would also include little sandwiches, mixed nuts and one of those aforementioned pickles. Coffee with Grandma is a meal.

Served, more often than not, on pretty china.

Grandma's pretty china is now beautifully stacked in my dining room buffet awaiting company. I put it to gracious use at every opportunity.

EIGHT

Grandma's favorite

MY GRANDPARENTS HAD FOUR children. When her oldest son procreated, Grandma became a grandma for the first time. That first granddaughter is my cousin Cheri. She would have the opportunity to get to know a younger Grandma than me.

"I have lots of memories of her younger, they are really scattered," Cheri remembers. "I helped bottle feed lambs with her. I remember chicken butchering time. She named all the dogs Shep. She always had a great garden."

Grandma exercised her grandmotherly chops on Cheri and her brothers. "She made us share the bath water with all taking a bath on Saturday night," Cheri said. "Fried eggs for breakfast cooked in oil, puffed rice or cornflakes as other options."

Cheri also has vivid memories of a set of trick birthday candles that didn't blow out, a prank I can imagine Grandma found immensely satisfying. "Those candles made me mad!" Cheri said.

An antique appliance is among Cheri's memories of Grandma. "She washed clothes with a wringer washing machine I think until she was quite old."

Grandma babysat for several teachers when she and Grandpa moved to town, and after Grandpa died, Grandma traveled with a lady called Melinda on several senior bus trips.

Eventually, Cheri would grow up to be one those teachers, and she would be the grandchild who would make Grandma into Great-Grandma.

> *February 18, 1985: February 18 is a special day for me as the 18th was Henry's birthday, but Cheri and Danny did a wonderful thing: They had a baby boy today, Samuel Patrick, weighing 8 pounds 11 oz. A nice little fatty. I was with Jim and Maggie to see them tonight so now I'm a great-grandma. The sewing club quilted Alvina's quilt today at Margaret's; it was very nice we got done.*

"She watched Sam and Hilary (Cheri's second child) for me during school year," Cheri said. "She taught them to string buttons and all the old nursery rhymes."

Here's how she recorded another great-grandchild's birth.

> *April 7, 1987: Had three kids [to babysit]: Jesse, Samuel and Logyn. Odin cam back from the Cities. I went there after kids left. I got a bed; he is moving to the Cities to live. Tim and Sherri had a baby boy today.*

She made haste to visit the baby, named Tavis.

> *April 12, 1987: Left at 8 with Jim's for the Cities to visit*
> *at Tim's to see the new baby. It is a very nice baby. Had*
> *breakfast in St. Cloud and supper in Little Falls. Got home*
> *at 7.*

Cheri and her brother Tim would make Grandma a great-grandmother several times before my younger sister Kay contributed with her first son, Drew. On Oct. 15, 1999, Grandma had this to say about Drew:

> *Bob called at 8 and said Kay had her baby, a boy, 6 pounds,*
> *9 ounces, named Andrew Curtis. … Ruth picked me up to*
> *go to center for birthday party. Sadie was 91. Was tired when*
> *I got home. Weather was nice. Bob called again and said baby*
> *was a cute little fellow.*

While I was writing Grandma semi-regularly from the far-flung locations to which I traveled for work, my cousin Cheri was cultivating a close adult relationship with Grandma which as special to both of them. After the babysitting years, Cheri would have coffee with Grandma weekly at her house, at her apartment and eventually at the elder care facility. Cheri was a good chauffeur, too.

> *August 16, 1990: Had a happy feeling when I woke up as*
> *Freda and I were going with Cheri to visit Mary [in Villard,*

Minnesota]. Left Cheri's at 9, stopped in Alexandria's for an hour and in p.m., we all went to Glenwood. Patrick babysat [his sister Paula]. I baked him a birthday cake; we had that when we came back from Glenwood.

Cheri is mentioned literally thousands of times in Grandma's diaries, but here's one typical month of mentions among many.

July 1, 1998: I decided to paint my bedroom today. It's hard work when one can't see. Got done at noon. I was so very, very tired. Cheri brought me a pail of strawberries.

July 7, 1998: Went to Freda's for morning coffee then to grocery store and then to eye doctor so have everything done. I also got my blood pressure pills: 100 for $4.99 so I can't complain on price. Tied a baby quilt in the p.m. Cheri was down in the night; brought me some juneberries. Will bake a pie tomorrow.

July 16, 1998: Cheri stopped in while I was hanging living room curtains on the clothesline. Said she would stop in p.m. and help me hang them.

July 23, 1998: Cheri picked Freda and I up at 9 to go to Perham shopping. Had morning coffee at the Gathering Grounds and noon lunch at the Station House. Also visited Bertha. She was very good. Got home at 3:30.

NINE

Aging & vanity

GRANDMA ONCE SAID SHE had only one regret in life.

During a visit with my cousin Paula, Grandma said her only regret was that she should have worn a padded bra when she was younger, because her dresses would have fit better.

Then after a little thought she added, "But that would be like false advertising!"

OK, bearing that in mind, I don't regret the natural padding I've added that past couple years. Please pass the ice cream.

"She also wasn't afraid to tell me yellow was not my color," Paula reported on the Facebook thread where this regret was revealed.

"Only my Aunt Laura!" said Grandma's niece, Diane. "She was always concerned about how she looks."

Indeed.

Grandma was a little bit vain. Not in a bad way—I admired this about her. Her earrings always matched her outfit, for instance, and she colored her hair into her 80s. It must have worked for her—she was never overweight, and she lived to 104. In fact, I dedicated my fitness memoir to her because "she proved vanity is a virtue."

During one autumn visit, I accompanied her and my dad to an appointment with her eye doctor. On the way home, she wanted to stop at a nearby shoe store because she was looking for a particular type of sandal—my 100-year-old grandmother was shoe shopping! How great was that?! I found it amusing when we couldn't find quite the right style of sandal and the sales lady helpfully suggested the sandal selection would be more plentiful in the spring. I only hoped my 100-year-old fashion-conscious grandma would be shopping for new sandals the following spring!

I found the following little essay tucked into one of her journals, which she began keeping when she was 70. It is titled "The Stranger" (a quick internet search revealed the author to be Rose Madeline Mula).

The Stranger

A very weird thing has happened. A strange old lady has moved into my house. I have no idea who she is, where she came from, or how she got in. ...

She is a clever old lady and manages to keep out of sight for the most part, but whenever I pass a mirror, I catch a glimpse of her. And whenever I look in the mirror to check my appearance, there she is, hogging the whole thing, completely obliterating my gorgeous face and body. This is very rude. I have tried screaming at her, but she just screams back.

The essay continues for several paragraphs describing how the Stranger "plays nasty games ...altering my clothes" and doing "something really sinister to the volume controls on my TV, radio and telephone. Now, all I hear are mumbles and whispers" and other mean tricks.

I found this amusing as I stood on the precipice of 50. There was a strange middle-aged lady in *my* house with a flabby butt and crow's feet who left marbles in my shoes and made it difficult for me to recall exactly the right word without a thesaurus.

I found a little comfort knowing Grandma felt this way at 70-something and yet, she was still going strong, getting her hair done, painting her nails and shopping for shoes.

That's the old lady I want to be. One who, despite being unable to unscrew a jar of spaghetti sauce, maintains a firm grip on her vanity and her sense of humor.

⌘

THROUGHOUT HER RETIREMENT, GRANDMA had her hair done once a week. She managed to sleep motionlessly on her back to preserve the curls as long as possible.

Grandma colored her hair until she was 85. Ah, the great debate: go gray naturally or fight it every step of the way.

Grandma landed firmly in the color camp. Gray hair makes you look like a grandma, after all, and while grandmas are good at making cookies and reading books, they're just not quite put together.

Grandma took a nap almost every day. She didn't call it "beauty sleep," but maybe that's what it was.

Grandma's attention to appearance began early.

"I talked with Alice Schoon to see if she could recall any memories and she remembered one instance where Laura was about 17," her cousin Alvina remembered. "When Alice and her mother Esther Windels were visiting, Laura's mother took one of Laura's blue ribbons and used it on young Alice's hair. Alice may have been about two. Laura was not too happy losing her blue ribbon to young Alice. Of course, this would have been one of Laura's memories that she relayed to Alice later in life. They laughed about it as they got older."

Well, if you're wondering when Grandma started feeling old, maybe it was when she turned 77 in 1992.

> *March 8, 1992: Was 7:25 when I woke up. I woke Mary and Donnie right away as we went to 8:15 services. Put an egg casserole in the oven before we left for breakfast, then had BBQ with us for dinner. Janice and Mike and baby also stopped in. Virginia, Bob and Freda stopped in from 3-6, and in the night I had 18 friends stop in. Was really tired when I went to bed.*

March 9, 1992: I felt like I had been rolled over by a roller when I woke up this morning but limbered up when I started moving around. Clarine came for coffee and in the p.m. Laurence stopped. Tried some of my new coffee and when he left, Nancy and Cheri stopped so had more coffee. The weather was cooler. Got five cards in the mail.

Despite her protestations, Grandma was an active septuagenarian and octogenarian.

March 8, 1995: A cold morning. I worked on my lunch for afternoon and night. I had nine for lunch in p.m. and eight in the night. A very nice day. Got nine cards in the mail. It's nice to be 80. Got many nice gifts. Got a plant from my prayer sister.

"I remember her birthday that year," Alvina said, "because she was 80 and got down on the floor to show me her cards and gifts she received. I always marveled at how spry and healthy she seemed to be."

⌘

AUNT MARY VISITED GRANDMA when she was 103 and a half at the elder care center, and Mary recorded Grandma reciting, from memory, the following poem by Mary Dow Brine, an American poet who died two years before Grandma was born. Grandma had a creaky, squeaky voice, at least in her later years, but to listen to her recite this poem is classic Grandma. She once told her cousin Alvina that a strong young man had assisted her similarly.

Somebody's Mother

The woman was old and ragged and gray
And bent with the chill of the winter's day.
The street was wet with a recent snow
And the woman's feet were aged and slow.
She stood at the crossing and waited long,
Alone, uncared for, amid the throng
Of human beings who passed her by
Nor heeded the glance of her anxious eyes.
Down the street, with laughter and shout,
Glad in the freedom of school let out,
Came the boys like a flock of sheep,
Hailing the snow piled white and deep.
Past the woman so old and gray
Hastened the children on their way.
None offered a helping hand to her
So meek, so timid, afraid to stir
Lest the carriage wheels or the horses' feet
Should crowd her down in the slippery street.
At last came one of the merry troop,
The merriest one of all the group;
He paused beside her and whispered low,

"I'll help you cross, if you wish to go."
Her aged hand on his strong young arm
She placed, and so, without hurt or harm,
He guided the trembling feet along,
Proud that his own were firm and strong.
Then back again to his friends he went,
His young heart happy and well content.
"She's somebody's mother, boys, you know,
For all she's aged and poor and slow,
"And I hope some fellow will lend a hand
To help my mother, you understand,
"If ever she's poor and old and gray,
When her own dear boy is far away.'
And "somebody's mother" bowed low her head
In her home that night, and the prayer she said
Was "God, be kind to the noble boy,
Who is somebody's son, and pride and joy!"

TEN

Brushes with death

GRANDMA LIVED INDEPENDENTLY UNTIL two weeks shy of her 100th birthday when she had a heart attack and double pneumonia.

That was her third brush with death, she would recall in her last years as she wondered aloud why she was still around. She made healthy choices throughout her life, eating right, getting regular exercise and driving carefully. When Grandma drank wine (I only ever saw her drink alcohol on holidays or special occasions), she drank a glass of Mogen David, a brand described as "sweet and tasty" that's been around almost as long as Grandma was having been established in 1933.

Though she was more stooped in later years, she remained in pretty good health through her 90s. I remain convinced I will live into my 90s or 100s because of her good Minnesota genetics (and those of my dad, her son Bob). She was severely hearing impaired, but closed captioning on the TV helped keep her abreast of current events, including political conventions which she found endlessly fascinating.

Grandma's first brush with death occurred when my parents got married in 1964. Mom grew up in western North Dakota, a full day's drive from where my father was raised in Minnesota. Here is how Grandma remembered the wedding in a memory album I made for my parents' 50th anniversary:

> *I was very sick with bleeding ulcers in the hospital so I couldn't go to the wedding. But three days before its date, I was discharged; though still very sick and weak, we decided to go. We stayed in a motel there; I didn't get any sleep as the young guys were making so much noise razzing Bob, so after the reception we decided to leave for home. I laid in the back seat, got home at 3 a.m. and went back to the doctor the next day. Then I found out they discharged me instead of the lady who should have been discharged so was back in the hospital again.*
>
> *And I'm still here.*

Breaking her neck was her second brush with death.

When she was 84, she fell off the steps inside her garage and broke her neck. Yes! Broke her neck! She actually got up and, feeling stupid for falling, went back inside the house!

My aunt Jean, Grandma's daughter-in-law, remembered it this way.

"The phone rang around 3:30 a.m. on July 20, 1999," Jean wrote. "It was Grandma Laura. When I answered, all she said was, 'Something happened to me,' and she hung up the phone."

Aunt Jean ran into the bedroom and woke up her husband, Grandma's son Wally.

When they got to Grandma's, there was note on the kitchen counter saying she had fallen off the garage step and hit her head on the car's wheel rim. She was sitting in the living room, fully dressed, with a folded-up towel supporting her neck. She held the towel with both hands.

Grandma told Wally and Jean that around 9 o'clock the night before, she had gone into the attached garage to lock the garage door. "She had been concerned someone was stealing gas, siphoning it from her car gas tank," Jean remembered. Grandma accidentally slipped on the top step into the house, feel backward and hit her neck.

"She said it hurt so bad, but she just didn't know what to do," Jean said. "She decided to go to bed, put on her pajamas and laid down."

The pain was so intense, she got out of bed, dressed in her regular clothes and tried to alleviate the pain by holding her neck with the towel.

Grandma insisted she did not want to ride in an ambulance, but my uncle, who had just completed first responder trainer, was not about to put her in his van. He and my aunt convinced Grandma to let them call 911 and request no lights or sirens.

The ambulance from the next-door town arrived, the emergency techs put a neck brace on Grandma, and they drove her to the emergency room.

"Dr. Paulson took an X-ray," Jean said. "He became very alarmed and said she fractured her C2 vertebrae."

Injuries to the cervical spine at the C1 and C2 vertebrae at the top of the neck are considered the most severe of all spinal cord injuries.

The X-rays techs had removed Grandma's hearing aids so she couldn't hear a word of this diagnosis until Wally and Jean convinced the doctor to put her hearing aids back in.

A helicopter was called, and Wally flew with Grandma to a more metropolitan hospital in Fargo, North Dakota.

Jean returned home to inform her school-age children and arranged for her own mother to take care of them so she could drive to Fargo. When Jean arrived, Grandma was still in the emergency room, but she eventually was admitted and moved to a standard room.

The doctors prescribed a halo, a device used to stabilize the cervical spine after a traumatic injury. The apparatus consisted of a halo vest, stabilization bars and a metal ring encircling the patient's head and fixated to the skull with multiple pins. The operating rooms were full, and the doctors did not want to risk delay so they decided to install it in her room.

"I knew I would not be able to watch, so I went to a family room, down the hall," Jean said. "Wally planned to stay, but when they walked in with a Black+Decker drill box, he looked a little pale, too. He later joined me in the waiting room, but we could hear them drilling."

July 20, 1999, also happened to be Jean and Wally's 25th wedding anniversary. After Grandma's halo was installed and she fell asleep, Wally and Jean slipped out to a nearby restaurant set in a remodeled train station for a quick dinner.

Imagine! An octogenarian with a metal halo! She couldn't turn her head, and I imagine it was no fun trying to sleep. In her diary, she described it as weighing eight pounds, and the tight vest was very uncomfortable. She could not shower while wearing the brace and she had to be wiped down with alcohol wipes to prevent skin sores. The worst part for her wasn't the pain or the fear of not healing—it was being embarrassed about her appearance. The woman who normally loved visitors didn't want to see anyone when she was wearing the brace for a couple of months, and she insisted absolutely no one take any photos. She didn't like looking strange. Well, who does? But you think you get over vanity by the time you're 84!

That attitude helped her get better, I think. She was stubborn, and she healed, and she went on to live another decade and a half on her own. Someone else cut from different cloth might have given up, suffered deteriorating health and died. Not Grandma.

Everyone pitched in to help Grandma. Her daughter Mary joined Wally at the hospital, where she stayed ten days. Someone stayed with her the first four nights back at home, and she then went back to living alone. "I got along fine," she reported in her diary.

My uncle Jim was reluctant to leave his mother alone. "The doc told us not to spoil her and she insisted she could stay alone," my aunt Mary remembered. A nurse came to Grandma's house daily to help, and one of her sons drove her back to Fargo every two weeks for check-ups.

As she became more comfortable with her situation, she relented to having visitors and even allowed a few photos. Her diary, which was left uncharacteristically blank for nine weeks, began to fill with reports of visitors. "My friends have been very good in dropping in for visits. I've had some on nearly every day." She even reported walking to church wearing her brace and taking communion in early October (her church was across the street by then).

Nearly three months after the fall, the doctor removed her halo and vest. "What a wonderful feeling. It really hurt by one back post," Grandma recorded her in diary. "Mary and I had soup (for supper), then Jim's, Bob's and Wally's stopped by. Everyone was happy. I wear a neck brace."

Aunt Jean remembers that for years, one could see the indentations in Grandma's head from the screws, but she lived long enough that they eventually faded. Besides wearing that ugly halo, those little dents were worst repercussions of her fall.

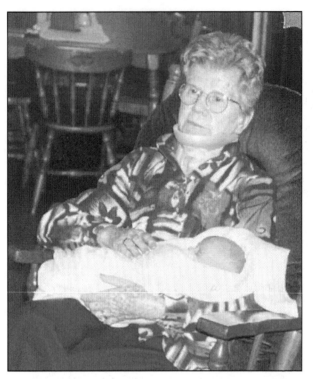

This picture of Grandma was taken when she was still wearing the neck brace. That's her great-grandson Drew in her lap; he was only nine days old. She wrote in her diary, "He is a nice little fellow, and they are happy with him."

"It truly was a miracle at age 84 she was able to heal so quickly and have no side effects from the accident," Jean said. "In fact, Wally used to say on occasion, it made her brain clearer! He would tease her, saying 'It shook all the cobwebs out.' This was an example of her strength and tenacity. She was a very determined lady."

ELEVEN

Loss

August 6, 1998: Got up early and washed and rolled my hair; when it got dry, I went for groceries. Freda, Virginia and Nancy had coffee in p.m., then we went to Haycreek, put flowers on Henry's and Art's graves. After that we had hamburgers at H.B.'s. Very good. Ended with a strawberry short cake at Nancy's.

More than most, Grandma was faithful. Her week revolved around going to worship services until she moved into elder care just shy of 100. An ardent Lutheran, she believed in the soul. That faith is what got her through the volume of grief only a 104-year-old experiences. She was a widow for forty-two years. Her daughter-in-law who lived two doors down for decades lost a battle to cancer. Two of her grandchildren died young. Her sisters. Her brothers. Her youngest son died when she was 102. So many friends and neighbors got to the finish line before she did.

"It's very quiet here and I don't have friends no more living, just two in the nursing home," she wrote in a letter in October 2014, one of her last to me. "I don't like fall; that's all death. Spring is better when everything comes alive."

One of the ways she paid tribute to those who had died was to visit their gravesites, almost always on Memorial Day. Early on in her retirement, she made these cemetery pilgrimages with her sister Freda. When Freda joined the throng of the dead, Grandma's son Wally accompanied her. When Wally could no longer do it, her daughter, Mary, performed chauffeur duties.

"I took my mother to four cemeteries yesterday," Mary reported on Facebook. "I took her to the grave sites of her husband, sister, two grandsons, a daughter-in-law and several of friends and family. She stood silently by each grave and shared no thoughts with me. Our last stop was the grave of her parents. It was an uphill climb, so I pulled the walker uphill and she walked behind. She shared stories about her parents and how happy her mother was when my brother was born. None of this was easy for Mom as she was in and out of the car several times, but it was a day where mom taught me about respect and I truly came away the winner."

⌘

LOSING HER HUSBAND WAS difficult, of course, and Grandma never forgot him. Sorrow followed the loss of any of her siblings, but perhaps most painful was Freda's death.

Freda was three years older, and they were so inseparable growing up that people called them "the Becker twins." They married brothers and lived on neighboring farmsteads until they moved into town. In one interview, Grandma described Freda as her best friend, a pal always willing to go along with anything. When they both were close to 80, Grandma and Freda cut their own Christmas trees in the ditch by a road.

Like Grandma, Freda faired well health-wise into her 80s and lived on her own. Reading between the lines of Grandma's diaries, she may have had a few mini-strokes in the months before she died.

> *July 21, 1998: Went to store and stopped at Nancy's. Jim was to pick me up at 5 to go to the funeral home in Glenwood for Geneva's memorial. Alvina stopped at the same time as Jim told me Freda was real mixed up. I told Alvina to go with Nancy, but Freda was better when Nancy got there. We also stopped by when we came home. She was OK. She's had a spell like this before.*

A few months later, Freda would be gone.

> *November 22, 1998: "Another nice day. Went to early church. After services, Harley and Verna took Freda and I, and we went to Detroit Lakes for breakfast. After that we went shopping at Kmart and on way home, we stopped at Eagles for ice cream. Truly a very nice day."*

November 23, 1998: Clarine came for coffee in p.m. I cleaned the two bedrooms for Thanksgiving. Tried to call Freda in p.m. different times, but never got an answer. Jim was here at 5; I asked him to check on her. He found her dead on her knees by the bed in her nightgown, so it seems like she died getting to bed for the night. Lights were all shut off. What a shock. Several relatives came here that night. Mary came home.

November 24, 1998: It's been a steady flow of friends here all day and a lot of good food bought in. [Freda's daughter] Virginia and Bob got here on time for noon lunch. I went with them to funeral home. Also picked out what she was to wear. The people kept coming. Funeral is Saturday at 1.

November 25, 1998: I had an 8 o'clock hair appointment, and at noon Virginia and Bob came for noon lunch before leaving for Elk River. I went to nursing home to tell Erna. When I got home, more people came. In the night, Mary and I went to church and had pie there after the services. The weather is perfect.

November 26, 1998: Thanksgiving. Mary and I got busy for our dinner. Donnie bought the turkey and gravy. Herman was with them. They all left about 3. Marla, her husband

and Bruce stopped in. They were on a walk. The night was very lonely and quiet. Weather was beautiful.

November 27, 1998: *Was alone this a.m. When I awakened, went to store early to get a few things. Clarine came for coffee which was nice. At 2:30, Jim picked me up and we went to funeral home to see Freda. She looked very natural—just sleeping. I went home again, and later Mary and I went and stayed till 8. Virginia's family came here for lunch. Very nice.*

November 28, 1998: *The weather has been very nice. Mary and I got things in order for a lunch at 11 as Mary Alice and Dwight and Lou Ann and Carol Louise were driving up to be here at 11. Also Bob's family. We walked across the street to the church at 12:30. Had a big crowd. I would guess 200. It was muddy at Hay Creek. Everyone has gone back to their home again.*

Looks like she wrote about the funeral again the next day, which would have been Sunday.

November 29, 1998: *We were busy getting the noon lunch ready. Wally brought a meat and cheese tray and bread. Lou Ann and Carol came first then Dwight and Mary Alice, Bob and Kay and Chuck, and Patrick and Paula. We all walked to church at 12:30. Many people, about 250.*

Everything went good. Was muddy going to Hay Creek. Mary left for home soon after we got home. Wally and Jim were here for a while. Weather was extra nice.

⌘

GRANDMA ALSO LIVED TO see two grandsons die. In 1984, the year before Grandma's first diary, Wally and Jean's third son Kip died three days after he was born.

In January 1999, a few months after Freda's death, my brother Curtis died in traffic crash caused by a snowstorm. Here's how Grandma recorded it and a few of the relevant days after.

> *January 17, 1999: Was raining a little when I went to church. Had snowed while we were there. Had to go back to clean up from communion. Had a T.V. dinner. Jim stopped in to help roll quilt. Dorothy called in the night to come for cards. Jerome was home. Had a nice time. Was snowing hard when we came home.*

> *January 18, 1999: Clarine came for coffee. While she was here, Bob and Karen stopped with the sad news that Curtis was killed in a car accident last night by Fargo. Only 26 years old. How sad. Jim and Wally also came. I went with Jim's to Bob's in p.m. They had many friends come and a lot of food. Mary and Paula came; said roads were very slippery.*

January 21, 1999 [day of funeral]: I made French toast for breakfast; Pat's girlfriend was with. Left at 10 for the church. The crowd was overflowing and so very, very sad. They served a nice dinner. I came back with Wally's as Mary's left for Villard. I've been very restless.

January 24, 1999: Went to early church. I took Christmas cookies for coffee. Harold and Jane stopped in at noon. Had lunch. They left at 2:30. Bob called; he and Karen are coming. I called Wally to come and Jim's came when they got home from the Cities. They are so thankful for friends.

When I shared these passages with Grandma's family on Facebook, they evoked memories with my aunt Mary: "Some memories stay so clear in your mind," she wrote. "I remember receiving the call at school and Paula and I driving on some snowy, icy roads to Wadena, and Monica, when we got to your place you were out shoveling the sidewalks. The day of Curtis's visitation Paula and I attended a funeral for a Minnewaska student that was also killed in a car accident and how the minister also included the family of Curtis Wallgren in his prayers."

⌘

AS I WAS BROWSING through Grandma's journals, I discovered Grandma's perspective of her daughter-in-law Maggie's bout with cancer and her death in 1992. Grandma first reported Maggie wasn't feeling well in the spring, and she mentioned Maggie almost every day for four months. I really debated whether or not I should create such a long section about it, but I decided it shows how upset Grandma was about Maggie's illness, and it also shows how our family is supportive in hard times (Grandma was babysitting regularly for Hilary, who is mentioned repeatedly; Hilary is Maggie's granddaughter).

April 1, 1992: April Fool! It was quiet although I did fool a few after church when we were having soup. Had 10 different kinds of soup. I had wild rice. Very good. I brought sandwiches and cake for the ACT [Active Christian Teens]. Jim stopped in after late services. Maggie still doesn't feel good.

April 11, 1992: Went to early church and Bible study. Had bars left from sale the day before (Patron's Sale). Freda went to second services. She stopped to look at new table and had soup with me, and in the p.m. Wally's family was down. We finished the soup for supper. I had also taken two bowls to Jim's as Maggie isn't feeling good.

April 28, 1992: Hilary went to school. I cleaned house while she was gone as I had asked Timie, Dorothy and Freda for casserole supper. Served it simple so wasn't too much work. Played two games of cards. Dorothy won both. I had been to Jim's; Maggie is still sick. Goes to see doc in Fargo Thursday.

April 29, 1992: Did some sewing and pressing and in p.m. I walked to Senior Citizens Center to quilt. Was home again at 4. Jim walked over after supper; Maggie surely isn't well. He said he would have someone till my garden and spray the dandelions soon.

May 1, 1992: Washed and rolled my hair. Went to church at 9 to set up for Mother-Daughter banquet. Worked till noon. Was tired when I got home so rested most of p.m. till Mary and Paula came. Jean and Betsy and Karen met here, and we all went together to the banquet. Was very nice. I stayed a little later. Jim was over and said things aren't very good for Maggie at the doctor's. They go to Fargo again on Monday.

May 4, 1992: Washed clothes before Hilary came. They dried real nice. Clarine came for coffee. Nancy also stopped with Valerie. Took Hilary to Wally's when I went to Erna's birthday. Had a nice lunch. Filled the car with gas and stopped at Dean's before I came home. Jim was here tonight. Said they are still running tests on Maggie. Was nice this p.m. Nancy said they made good selling lunch at Louie Lund sale Saturday.

May 5, 1992: Hilary went to school. I also took a box for Boys Town Truck. Then I went to Connie's for my manicure I got from Mary for Mother's Day. It was nice just sitting *and having someone doing it. Stopped a few minutes at Freda's to tell her it surely sounds like Maggie has cancer. She has two tumors in her head. She will start treatment in near future.*

May 10, 1992: Mother's Day. Made a shipwreck before I went to church. Also went to Bible study and helped Viola wash coffee pots. Baked a fresh rhubarb cake and the three boys all were home today. Also Freda. Poor Maggie. Had trouble walking but had been to church this morning when Jim was fishing. It turned quite cool towards evening. Mary called after the rest had left.

"I remember that when we went to Laura's for Mother's Day Maggie had unexplained pain in one leg and things just went from bad to worse from there," my mother remembered.

May 11, 1992: Washed clothes and had them hung on the line when Hilary came. Clarine came for coffee. Went to Dorothy's to stitch on quilt. After Hilary left, Jim stopped in at 7. He just got home from Fargo. He took Maggie to the hospital. They will run more tests. I mowed lawn for 1½ hours. Clarine called; said that Bessie passed away today. It was also her birthday and anniversary.

I feel compelled to remind readers that Grandma was 77 when she mowed her lawn for an hour and a half.

May 12, 1992: *Mary called early. Wally had called her last night [saying] that Maggie was in hospital in Fargo. I took Hilary to school at 9 and then took doughnuts and coffee to Dorothy. Also quilted on the quilt. Picked Hilary up when I came home. Cleaned garage. Also swept basement. Lawrence stopped in. Had Jim for supper. He called tonight; he had talked to Maggie, but she didn't know anything.*

May 13, 1992: *Washed my hair this morning and did some wash outside, and at 2:30 we went to the community home to visit Ethel, Orville and Leona. Leona is moving to nursing home in the near future. Then we went to the funeral home to see Bessie and visit with relatives. Jim stopped in when he came from Fargo, but still didn't know anymore of Maggie.*

May 14, 1992: *Made a hotdish for Bessie's funeral which was at 11. Rode with Kenny and Charlotte out to Haycreek [Cemetery]. It didn't look very nice out there. Ruth picked me up for cards at the center in the night. Had eight tables. A very good lunch. Sadie and her daughter served. Haven't heard anything of Maggie today.*

May 15, 1992: *Gathered up the garbage and put it on the curb this morning. Was a beautiful quiet morning but still dry, and at 10:30, I walked across to church for Kinsey and Hilary's Grandparents Day. It was nice. Had a nice lunch at noon, and at 2 I went to Senior Citizens for the May birthdays. Ruth has one tomorrow. Had a nice lunch there, too. Went to Wallace garage sale; bought a sugar spoon that matched my set. Stopped at Lawrence and Nancy's for a few minutes. Jim went to see Maggie. He stopped when he came home. The Dr. says Maggie has cancer of liver, but they haven't taken test yet. Forecast is for rain.*

May 19, 1992: Hilary went to school, and I went stitching at Dorothy's and in p.m. I finished planting the garden. A very windy day. Freda stopped a few minutes later in the p.m. Jim stopped in; still no news on Maggie.

May 20, 1992: Went up town for a haircut and check-up at the dentist and in p.m. went to sewing at Dorothy's, and at 9:30, Jim stopped in when he came from visiting Maggie with bad news. She has cancer all over. The fast kind and can do nothing for it. I feel so badly. She is such a nice person.

May 21, 1992: Went up town to mail out my tax form. Had to make a couple tries. Didn't stop anywhere. Was still feeling bad about Maggie. Freda stopped in during the p.m. I didn't go to cards tonight.

May 22, 1992: Was raining when I got up. Lawrence and Nancy stopped in, mostly talked of Maggie. After they left, I went uptown to pay electric bill and take my check to the bank and in p.m. Lawrence, Nancy, Charlotte and I were to Freda's for strawberry pie. Stopped at Jim's on way home.

Maggie was home but very miserable. Forecast is for frost; it had rained nearly ½ inch.

May 24, 1992: *Went to early church and had coffee as Red Frustic was our speaker this month. And at 11 Freda and I drove out to Orin's for brunch and watched the young couple open gifts [day after Jodie Petersen wedding]. Got home at 2:30. Just rested the rest of the day. Took a dish to Jim's to bake for breakfast. Maggie seemed to be good.*

May 26, 1992: *Went to Freda's quilting when Hilary was in school; picked her up at noon and went to Eagle's for noon lunch and then to Freda's again; quilted till 3, then went home. I had coffee for Cheri and kids, also Lawrence. Jim stopped in the night; things are the same.*

May 27, 1992: *Mary drove up. Got here about 10:15. Had coffee, then we drove to Haycreek to pick up the flowers. Went to Sebeka for noon lunch. Very good. In p.m., we went to craft store and to Wally's to show them the housecoat Mary brought for them to give Maggie—a pretty lavender. Then we stopped at Freda's. Ruth was there quilting and when we got back here, we walked to Jim's. He was alone. Cheri and Maggie weren't home yet from Fargo, but as we were leaving, they came but we didn't stop. Jim came and asked Mary to stop in, so she did, and then we went to Bob's for supper. We had a busy day.*

May 28, 1992: Kenny Becker stopped for coffee; also Lawrence came so they were here nearly two hours. Was a nice day. Lawrence mowed in p.m. I baked bread, cake and coffee cake for bake sale at Senior Citizens. Verna stopped in. She had brought soup to Jim's and at 7:30, I went to graduation for Kinsey and Hilary. It was very nice. Had coffee and bars after Jim left. Maggie in hospital in Fargo.

May 29, 1992: Washed my hair and rolled it when I got up. Made a salad to take for potluck dinner. Went for dinner early, intending to buy at the bake sale but everything was gone. Had a good dinner. I quilted till 1:30, then I went to Karen Dreyer's to look at some of Jody's clothes. I bought three blouses and a dress. Had coffee there. Mowed the corners, etc., when I got home. Jim stopped in when he got home from Fargo. Maggie was the same.

May 31, 1992: I overslept. Woke up at 3 minutes till 8. Church is at 8:15, but I made it. Also got my cookies and sweet bread there, and at 11:30 I went with Jim to see Maggie. Her legs were somewhat better. She was good to visit with. Got home again at 5:30. Took a little nap when Wally's stopped in. Mary Grant called but didn't come when I had company. I have the table set for my company tomorrow.

June 1, 1992: I had Maggie on my mind so much when I got up, but I had to get busy as today Goldie, Mary Winther and friend Wanda were coming for noon lunch. Nancy brought meatballs; Charlotte, salad; and Freda, strawberry pie. I furnished the rest. Really had a nice visit with them. Goldie had failed a little. We all walked across to the church for them to see. Cheri called me. Jim was staying overnight with Maggie as she had fallen in the a.m.

June 2, 1992: *Clarine came for coffee and Mary Grant also stopped in after she served vacation Bible school kids cookies in the p.m. I made potholders, and pressed towels for shower gift. Jim stopped in at 5. He just came from Fargo. Said Maggie was some better. Poor thing. I feel so bad. Hope we get rain.*

June 8, 1992: *Washed clothes before Clarine came. Had Hilary while Cheri took Maggie to Fargo for treatment and after Hilary left, I went to the Senior Center to water flowers and put up the sign. Stayed and quilted a little. Jim came after supper; felt bad about Maggie. Wally also came to till garden. Jedd was going to a Mills ballgame Tuesday. Jim and I each gave him $5. I also went to Ruth's for smear [a card game]. The weather has warmed up a little.*

June 9, 1992: *Got up early and gave myself a perm. Was done at 8:30. At 9, I walked to Jim's to have coffee. One wouldn't know Maggie; she is so puffed. Jim was taking her* *for last treatment in the p.m. Freda called me to come for strawberry pie with Helman Allen. Very good.*

June 10, 1992: Went to dentist at 9. Was there 1 ½ hours. Karen, Monica and Steve stopped in for noon lunch. Monica is up to be bridesmaid for a friend's wedding. After they left, I painted a little on the trim on the front of the house. Walked to Jim's in the evening. Maggie seemed to be pretty good. She is sleeping better now. The weather was warm, and it is very dry.

I don't specifically recall this visit, but the friend who was getting married was the woman who would be my maid of honor twice, Jill. I did not see Maggie when I was home (I was living in Ohio at the time), and because I was in Minnesota for the wedding, I didn't come back for Maggie's funeral.

June 13, 1992: I walked to Mary's for our ride uptown. Also walked home again and picked some wild roses for Maggie. And at 12:30, I walked to Nancy's as she was grilling pork chops. Took a cabbage salad, and in the night I had Nancy, Charlotte, Freda, Ruth and Dorothy for cards. Lawrence is in Canada fishing.

June 15, 1992: Got up to a dark morning. It started to rain lightly at 11; nearly a half inch so that was good. Clarine was here for coffee. Cheri and Hilary also stopped in at the time. I made Jell-O for Maggie. Stopped in with it; she was sleepy. Also took radishes to cards and went to the center to help recycle cards. Played one game of cards after. Jim stopped a few minutes in the night. It was cool today.

June 17, 1992: *A rainy morning; had 1½ inches during the night. Went uptown for groceries but they were out of turkey breast; told me to come back in the morning. Maggie went by ambulance to Fargo today. Jim stopped tonight. She is not very good. Clarine stopped in after choir practice tonight. It rained ³/₁₀ of an inch during the day. Went to sewing at Erna's.*

June 18, 1992: *Jim stopped in. Said he called hospital and they said they couldn't wake her. Doc told him to let the family know but when he stopped last night, he said she was a little more alert. Bob and Karen were here when he stopped. Nancy and Phyllis were here in p.m. I went to center for a good beef roast supper. Also worked in garden a little. Planted a few marigolds in Jim's flower bed. Didn't have rain today but forecast is for more tomorrow.*

June 19, 1992: *Washed my hair. Is a very wet, damp day and in p.m. I went to the center for June birthdays. Also took a towel and holder to the craft store. Clifford Hemphill played. Jim stopped in the night. Maggie was much more alert in the p.m.*

June 20, 1992: Jim stopped in. He had called hospital. They said Maggie was having a temp. They are going at noon. I drove uptown. We also went to the Culture Building; looked very nice. And at noon we went to the center for stew; very good. And in the p.m. I worked in the garden. At 6, I went to Freda's and we watched the parade. Jim stopped in night. Maggie is about the same. I mowed the front lawn after I got home from parade.

June 23, 1992: Woke up Mary's family here. They left at 8:30 for Duluth. After I had washed the breakfast dishes, I decided to wash clothes. They dried real good. Went to the clinic for my new lenses; I think they are much better. Went to Freda's in the night for cards. Maggie is about the same.

June 24, 1992: I went to the center to get my quilt and [quilt] stand. Had coffee. After I got home, Eunice called that she would come at noon for lunch. Ruth also called that she would pick me up to go see the Rohn baby, and Phyllis called for me to come for supper. Grant's, Freda, Lawrence and Nancy were also there. Stopped at Jim's when I came home. Pastor Benson was also there. Jim said Maggie seemed better, and that they would start chemo on Friday. Wouldn't it be nice if she got better?

June 25, 1992: Took my walk and at 8:10, I went to the community action to help hand out [government] commodities.

It was very good this time. Got home early. Had coffee at Freda's when I brought [commodities] to her. Washed my hair as soon as I got home and in p.m., I went to center to work on cards. Jim was still happy when he got home. Maggie starts her treatment tomorrow. She seems better.

June 26, 1992: *Had a lot of drop-ins in the a.m. Clarine, Jim, Tim, Bob and Nancy went to potluck dinner. Also got a haircut at 11:30. Did my shopping in p.m. Rev. Bensen also stopped in for coffee, and in the night, Lawrence and Nancy picked Freda and I up to go to banquet at Blue Horizon. A real nice night. Called Jim when I got home; Maggie still seems to be OK and not sick from the chemo treatment.*

June 27, 1992: *Cheri brought Hilary when she went to Fargo, so I drove myself uptown, but she was good at the bakery. It was 3:30 before Cheri picked her up again. Maggie still seems to be a little better. Jim said she wants to come home, but she is still very weak. Greg Esala got married today. There also has been many working by the church for tomorrow's [centennial celebration]. It has been cool.*

June 29, 1992: *Washed clothes as soon as I got up, then took my walk around the church. Clarine came for coffee, and at 12:30 I went to church to fold newsletters, and at 3:30 I stopped at Lawrence and Nancy's when I went to the store* *for groceries; I asked them for breakfast tomorrow. Jim stopped at 9 on his way home from Fargo. Things still sound better; they plan to move her to Perham tomorrow. Forecast is frost in the north.*

June 30, 1992: *Had Lawrence, Nancy and Freda for breakfast. Wallace Brunning had called Freda, saying that they were stopping in, and Lorna would be along so they came here at 10:45. I had made caramel rolls in the morning so we had them again, and in p.m. Freda and I rode with them to Harold's; they were looking for records of the Brunnings. Got home again at 4:30, then Jim stopped. Maggie came to Perham today. I hope things go far better.*

July 1, 1992: *Baked cookies, a new recipe—not too special. Freda called and said she was having a picnic at her place the Fourth. Called for Mary to come for coffee but didn't get an answer. Charlotte called for me to come for strawberry pie this p.m., and it was very good. Jim stopped in when I got home; things still are good with Maggie at Perham. A very cold, damp day; rained 1½ inches last night.*

July 3, 1992: *I called Freda; we would go to Perham to see Maggie, but just got on the road when Wally stopped to tell me Jeannie was going picking berries so I came back and went with her; picked three five-quart pails of nice berries, and in the night, Wally's came to see the fireworks. Was real cool.*

July 4, 1992: Fourth of July: Went to Freda's for a picnic. Had quite a few there, and good food. At 2, I went to Perham to see Maggie. She was good; had a nice visit. Went back to Freda's and in the evening, I froze twelve containers of strawberries and got some ready for canning tomorrow so was tired when I was ready for bed. The weather was cool.

July 8, 1992: Took my walk and worked in the garden. A very nice morning. And at 1, I picked Clarine and Freda up and we went to Perham to see Maggie. The poor girl. She has painful sores in her mouth, but she was nice to visit with. Also visited Bertha at the nursing home and stopped uptown. Wally came down in the night and tilled the garden. Jim also stopped.

July 10, 1992: A very dark morning. Rained ¾ of an inch during the night. I made a potholder and went to the Senior Center for a few minutes, and at 12, I picked up Freda and Chris and went to Perham for dinner. It rained very hard and my car leaked. I went to see Maggie a few minutes. Stopped at center when we got back. Dorothy and I went to funeral home to see Ham Mueller; funeral is tomorrow. Canned 7½ quarts of peaches in the night.

Though she might freeze and can this much produce in other years, I'm imagining she did a lot of this in the summer of 1992 because it took her mind off her worries.

July 12, 1992: *Went to early church. Also had coffee, then went home and made breakfast for Mary Alice and Dwight, Freda and Christopher. They left at noon to go to Phelps Mill. Wally's family stopped by in the evening. Also Jim, when he came home from hospital. Maggie doesn't get any better.*

July 15, 1992: *Baked a pie to send home with Mary when she comes today. Got here at 2. We went to Perham to see Maggie. Had a nice visit, then shopped for one hour; bought a back-zip dress. Mary also got some things. Came back to Eagles for supper with Jim before he left to see Maggie. She left for home again at 8. Had a nice day.*

July 17, 1992: *Took my walk; stitched on a baby quilt I have on the frame. Cheri and kids walked here while Gene changed oil in car. Lawrence also stopped, and after noon, I went to Senior Center for birthday party. I also asked the smear ladies for cards in the night. A cool day. Jim and Maggie went to Fargo; she checked pretty good.*

July 18, 1992: *Phyllis picked me up for coffee; had a big crowd at coffee. Faye also was with us, and in p.m. canned 10½ pints of apricots. Bob and Karen stopped in the night; they had been to see Maggie, but they said Maggie was so sleepy.*

July 20, 1992: Took my walk and wrote Mary before I cooked coffee for Clarine. Was a very cool morning and in p.m. I sewed binding on the baby quilt, and at 5:30 I went to Nancy's to babysit Beck's baby while Nancy was to Ty's picnic at Finn Creek. Watched video of Valerie's wedding while she was gone. Phyllis also stopped in. Called Jim about Maggie when I got home; things don't sound too good. Also rendered lard I got from Tim's; I didn't know it was already rendered till I took it from oven. What a fool.

July 21, 1992: Washed and rolled my hair and took my walk. Washed dining room curtains; also the ones in my bedroom. And in p.m., Jedd came to mow the lawn, but the handle broke on the lawn mower. Wally took it to Brill and had it welded, so finished it in the night. Jim went to meeting in Alexandria. Cheri went to see Maggie; doesn't sound like she is very good. Cheri and kids were here in p.m.; they had been picking blueberries.

July 22, 1992: Went uptown to buy groceries. Went to Freda's at 10:30 for lunch with the Darkalls; celebrated our birthdays. Had a nice time. We all got gifts. Had an oil change on the car and went quilting at the center in the p.m. Jim stopped and said Maggie is not good.

July 23, 1992: Rolled my hair and took my walk when Lawrence called and said he would pick me up to go berry *picking. Picked two pails strawberries and enough blueberries for a couple pies. Got home; it was nearly 1 so hurried and ate and went to the center to work on cards, and when I got home Mary called and said Rosalie had died on the operation table; I felt so bad. Mary Grant was down in the night. Jim stopped and said Maggie wasn't good.*

July 24, 1992: Clarine came early to pick me up to go to rummage sale; wasn't much good. She stopped for coffee, and in the p.m. I got my hair cut, and then I went to the Senior Center for bingo. I got a nice tea set. Went to some more rummage sales. Met Jim after coming home. He said Maggie is very sick, and the kids would come home. He stopped again at 9. She was the same. He feels so bad.

July 26, 1992: Maggie passed away today. She had been so sick. I feel so sorry for the family. She was only 51. I went to early church and baked a blueberry pie when I got home. Steve and Holly walked here in the p.m. and told me Maggie had died. Wally's were over; also Freda and Bob's. They weather was nice today.

July 29, 1992: The day of Maggie's funeral. A nice cool day. Over 400 people. Many beautiful flowers. We opened the cards tonight; the memorials were $2,482.00. She is buried on the lot next to Wally's. So many of their friends drove up from the Cities. Mary's family left about 3, then

Wally's family came for a little while, so it was a long day,
and I'm tired as I prepare for bed tonight.

Maggie's daughter Cheri gave birth to her third child Erik in November of that year, so Cheri was pregnant through all of this, which strikes me as an extra difficulty at the time (though I remember being really happy my nephew Drew was born before the first Christmas we would have celebrated without Curt so maybe Erik's birth mitigated sorrow a bit).

"Yes, I can't tell you much about this pregnancy," Cheri said. "I don't remember a ton about this, but I always wondered if I spent enough time with my mom. According to this, I may have spent a lot of time with her. It was a hard time, but it appears Grandma helped me out quite a bit, too. Even though these memories are hard, it is good to think about her. Thanks."

In her Christmas card to me that year, Grandma wrote, "On Thanksgiving it was really a nice day. So many siting at one table, but we do miss Maggie so much at this holiday season, and I know is it hard for Jim, too."

⌘

GRANDMA WAS ABLE TO make her annual cemetery sojourn for the last time when she was 102, visiting the graves of Curt, Kip, Maggie and, most sad, her son Wally, who died the previous autumn.

"Donnie and I took Mom to three cemeteries today," my

aunt Mary reported in May 2017. "It was a big morning for her, but I know it was special for her. She was so tired when we got back that she wanted to take a nap, and when Donnie and I had lunch we could pick something up for her that she could eat after her nap. If I earned one point toward heaven, Donnie earned two!"

⌘

WHEN I ASKED FAMILY to share memories of Grandma, Alvina Kytta enthusiastically agreed. Alvina is mentioned frequently in Grandma's journals as a visitor. She is Grandma's first cousin once removed. "Laura's mother Augusta Windels Becker was my grandfather Fred Windels' sister," Alvina explained. "My mother was Aleda Windels Limanen and a first cousin to Laura. So that makes me a first cousin once removed to Laura. But through the years, Laura has felt more like an aunt to me."

"After my mother passed away in March 1977 when I was only 22 and the mother of a one-month-old baby," Alvina continued. "I needed people in my life to fill that empty spot. Laura was one of those people. Laura was also suffering that same year because she lost Henry in October 1977. My cousin Alice Windels Schoon lost her mother Esther in 1977 also. It was a tough year. Alice's dad was Harry Windels and was Laura's first cousin. We were a close-knit community back when I was growing up. We all lived within a few miles of each other. So Laura had known us all of our lives. She was my sister

Jeannette's Godmother."

Grandma remembered Alvina's birthday on January 10 nearly every year without fail, inviting her over for coffee to celebrate another year. Here's Grandma's memories from the turn of the century.

> *January 10, 2000: I asked Alvina to stop for coffee for her birthday today. It was snowing so hard I thought perhaps she wouldn't stop but she did. It's still snowing now at 9:30, our first real snowstorm this year and 5.5 inches of snow.*

Alvina contributed the following tribute to Grandma (written May 8, 2019).

Memories of Laura

Strolling past a small, neglected cemetery not far from my home, thoughts of those who were buried there trickled into my mind. Surrounded by a wire fence in the middle of a pasture, cows feeding on newly grown grass outside its perimeters, I remembered only one visitor that ever went there—Laura! For some years, she had been unable to go. But I remember when she would annually visit this poor neglected little place.

Somewhere in my collection of papers, I had kept some information about that cemetery. A local Shining Stars 4-H Club had taken on the project to keep the cemetery in better repair. They even placed a sign with the name of the cemetery. They mowed the grass, planted a few spruce trees and for a few years made it look appealing. They had even interviewed some of the local citizens about the people who were buried there. Luke Allen was one, along with Laura Wallgren. They told about one whole family who had succumbed to the 1918 flu pandemic. There were perhaps fewer than twenty graves. Some had markers written in either Swedish or Norwegian.

One zealous mower had decided it would be easier to mow if all the stones were in one place and proceeded to move them into a pile. This created quite a stir, as these stones marked the graves. Now it is not exactly known where the graves are located.

Another year, it was decided to try burn the grass to more easily see the markers. One of the spruce trees also went up in flames.

So who did Laura visit every year? She had a baby brother buried in that cemetery. Each year she would remember him and visit his unmarked grave. An unforgettable moment in time for a mother who lost her baby, grief that only fades in time, remembered by a sister each year.

Laura has now rejoined her family and is undoubtedly experiencing great joy meeting her baby brother, her mother and all those dear to her heart. Their once-sorrowed lives suffering grief, agony and death have been replaced with peace, life and love. Spending eternity with the One who knew all too well the suffering, pain, grief and death has given them a precious gift of peace, joy and eternal life.

TWELVE

Politics

GENERALLY, CENTENARIANS CAN GET away with things the rest of us can't.

Talking about politics in polite company, for example.

I enjoyed a lively visit with Grandma when she was 98, and at some point in the conversation (I believe it was right after her praise for the *Biography* episode on John Tyler, U.S. president from 1841-45), she observed that she'd lived through the terms of seventeen U.S. presidents (in the end, she survived eighteen).

Grandma was born in 1915, about halfway through World War I when Woodrow Wilson was president.

I marvel about that. She was alive when Woodrow Wilson was president. Women did not have the right to vote when my grandmother was born in 1915; the 19th Amendment was ratified in 1920.

A resident of Otter Tail County known to have voted Republican in every presidential election since 1936, Grandma remarked that her favorite presidents were Franklin Roosevelt and Bill Clinton. Before you dismiss her as a hopeless liberal, she said this about Barack Obama: "I don't know about him."

I think she still had not forgiven him for ruining the chances at the time of Hillary Clinton to be the first woman in the highest public office in the land which, for a woman who had seen a parade of sixteen other men through the Oval Office during her lifetime, probably would have been a nice change of pace.

Whatever her politics, it was impressive that my country school educated grandmother—who still lived by herself at the time (with some help)—followed politics and could form valid opinions about goings-on in Washington.

She struggled with poor hearing and failing eyesight, but she remained lucid and aware of current events. For example, after chatting with her during an Easter gathering in 2011, I noted in my blog that she was no more impressed with Donald Trump's presidential aspirations than I was. That remark would have come in the presidential election cycle *before* the one Trump won, which means she was paying attention to Republican *primary* debates, something only die-hard politicos do.

Having persevered through a tough election cycle recently, I went through Grandma's journals in 2000, when it took more than two months for George W. Bush to be declared the winner over Al Gore in the presidential race.

November 7, 2000: Election Day. Overslept. I washed clothes, had a lot, too. Jim stopped in. I told him I wasn't going to vote as I didn't know who to vote for. In p.m., I stopped to see Nancy, Valerie and kids, also got groceries. Clara stopped in after she voted. Got up at 2 a.m.; still didn't know who our president is. Forecast is for snow.

November 8, 2000: *Wrote Mary before I did any other thing. Froze some apples and covered up some in the garage as they say it will get cold tonight. I'm going with Jim's to Cheri's for Erik's birthday, which was last Friday. Had birthday cake and ice cream. Election was the main topic. Still don't know if Bush or Gore will be our next president.*

Grandma spent the next two months as she always did: Visiting, quilting, packing away harvest bounty (*lots* of apples), coping with cold and snow, attending church. She celebrated Thanksgiving with her daughter Mary's family, with drop-by visits from son Jim and son Wally's family. She tried a new recipe and didn't like the results.

November 28: *Been trying to find a good nut bread recipe. Decided to try one I had yet from Aunt Alma. It called for dates. I used raisins so [that] may be the reason it wasn't like I expected.*

She baked several batches of cookies. She won six cents at penny bingo one very cold day in early December. And on December 12, the day Bush was declared president, she attended two Christmas parties, one at the nursing home with her sister-in-law Charlotte and one with her sewing club. But she didn't mention Bush's accomplishment. She was living her life, confident that Washington, D.C., would sort itself out and not losing sleep about how it would do so.

> *January 20, 2001: A cold morning. I drove uptown for coffee. Watched the inauguration of President Bush before I went, and when I got home, made cookies and a pie in p.m. as Mary and Donnie are coming for dinner.*

THIRTEEN
April Fools' Day

GRANDMA HAD A GOOD sense of humor, and she loved practical jokes, especially if she was the prankster.

April Fools' Day is a major holiday on my father's side of the family. Grandma used to love playing April Fools' jokes, and my dad still loves to tease people.

I dug through her April first entries in search of proof of her foolishness. Among entries about lunch, ironing, quilting and visitors, she rarely failed to note it was April Fools' Day, though in 1998 when seven inches of snow fell and 2009 when a foot of the white stuff fell, the weather trumped all fun.

Have I mentioned Grandma lived in north central Minnesota, where winter is six months long if it's a day?

In the '80s, April Fools' Day was mentioned frequently with her brother-in-law's birthday.

1985: April Fools' Day and Odin's birthday. We celebrated his birthday with the neighbors coming, too. It was a very nice afternoon.

In other years, she only mentioned who she fooled, not how. In 1986, it was my cousin Cheri (Grandma's oldest grandchild). In 1991 and 1993, it was her friend Clarine. In 1992: "It was quiet although I did fool a few after church when we were having soup." In 2004, she mentions she fooled her niece, Virginia.

In 1996, the lack of fooling got noted: "Cloudy cool day. I didn't do any April fooling."

But when Grandma does bother to go into detail about the day's foolishness, I just have to chuckle.

> *1991: April Fools' ... Was a nice day. The New Horizon had a goat they would deliver for $10. Mary called to have one delivered to both Jim and Wally. They blame me for telling Mary.*

This joke reminded me of my uncle Wally's sense of humor (and is proof of the foolishness on this side of the family!). He and Grandma exchanged pranks regularly:

> *1994: April Fools'. I fooled Wally with a letter. It makes me happy. I did get him!*

> *1995: April Fools'. Wally planned to fool me, so I locked the garage door. He was here but couldn't get in.*

> *1997: April Fools' Day. I never fooled anyone. Wally came when I was gone and put the bench on top of the car.*

For me, I think April Fools' Day jokes are most funny when they're played on someone else. When someone pulls a joke on me, well, not so much.

Researchers have found apes laugh, dogs laugh, and babies laugh before they learn any other language. Laughter is pretty much the same across languages, and it has the same cadence for everyone—if you "ha, ha, ha" too fast or too slow, it's panting or, er, something else.

So, laughter is like sleep. We all do it instinctively, and *no one* really knows why. Maybe it's *God's* joke. In any case, a good laugh is good for the soul, which may explain Grandma's longevity.

FOURTEEN
Winter

THE BITTER COLD SNAP we endured in the Midwest during the winter before Grandma died got me wondering about how I recorded it in my diaries when I was in high school in Minnesota in the 1980s. A little detective work revealed that the coldest wind chill ever recorded in Minnesota was 71 degrees below zero on January 9 and 10, 1982.

Here's how 15-year-old me recorded it:

> *Dear Diary, (Dateline: 1/10/82)*
> *Today is Sunday and all weekend it has been bitterly cold. We played a BB game against Aitkin on Friday, but we lost miserably. We are a rotten team. I don't think we'll ever improve.*

To be honest, I wrote more about which boys I interacted with each day, and I rarely remarked on the weather, so this mention means the terrifyingly cold weather really merited it.

While I was rooting around for my old diaries, I came upon the diaries I inherited from my grandmother and in which the weather played a prominent role interspersed between mentions of her visitors and her daily activities.

A little more research revealed Embarrass, Minnesota, perpetually in the temperature cellar, recorded the coldest ever Minnesota temperature in January at 57 degrees below zero on January 21 and 22, 1996; the lowest February temperature ever recorded in Minnesota was 60 below zero on February 2, 1996 in Tower, Minnesota. Grandma lived about 200 miles southwest of Embarrass and Tower, but I figured it was probably very cold in her neck of the woods, too. I learned it was. Here are her weather-related entries for two weeks in late January and early February 1996. They reveal a lot about how Minnesotans persevere through what many other American consider ridiculous weather.

> *January 18, 1996: Woke up to a white world. I'm really snowed in. Jim stopped in on the snowmobile at 10:00. He was also snowed in but Maynard [a friend I'm guessing] opened our driveways tonight but it is still blowing. Forecast is for cold, so I painted the kitchen walls today. Everything looks nice and clean; if only I could keep it so. Card party was cancelled tonight, too. No school.*

January 19, 1996: Was 30 below when I got up this morning. Stayed cold all day. Will be as cold tomorrow morning, too.

January 20, 1996: It wasn't as cold as I expected. About 21 below.

January 25, 1996: Bitter cold. I worked on my quilt mostly. Started to sew it together. It will look nice.

January 26, 1996: Plugged the car in as soon as I got up as I had an appointment at Donna's at 9 [Donna was Grandma's hairstylist]. Was 23 below. Stopped at [her sister] Freda's after. ... Forecast is for cold all week.

My grandmother was using a block heater even though she parked her car inside an attached garage!

January 27, 1996: Plugged in the car when I got dressed as it's my turn to drive for coffee. ... Was to go with Wally's to Mary's tomorrow but Mary called and said forecast is bad, so we won't go. [In normal weather, Mary lived about 45 minutes away.] I had a dessert started but will take it to quilting Monday.

January 28, 1996: I walked to early church. Weather wasn't too bad; snowing lightly. After Bible study, [friend] Ruth asked me to go with her uptown for breakfast. Had French toast. Was snowing hard when we came home. I stayed put. Called Mary at 4. They had lots of snow and still snowing.

January 29, 1996: *Very cold and stormy. ... [Friend] Maynard Falk opened my driveway by 6 in the night. Surely have a lot of snow.*

January 30, 1996: *The weather has been bitter cold and I've been rather nervous as today I was to go to my eye doctor to see if he would pass me for my driving because he said I was on the borderline but he did pass me. ... I was surely happy I can drive some.*

Grandma was 80 in January 1996.

January 31, 1996: *Bitter cold. Kept busy all day as Wally's and Freda were coming for supper for Kinsey's birthday. Everyone ate good so I'm glad; not too much leftover. Forecast is for very cold tonight.*

February 1, 1996: *32 below. I wondered if there would be Ladies Aid but there were 25 ladies. ... They canceled school for tomorrow on account of the cold. Card party was also canceled tonight.*

February 2, 1996: *Very cold. Stayed home all day. Sewed a little on my quilt. The governor closed all schools for today.*

February 3, 1996: Was 30 below when I got up. ... Forecast is for a little warmer.

By February 9, she noted that "weather was beautiful." I don't know what "beautiful" meant, but I'm going to guess the sun was shining and the temperatures were closer to zero than 20 below.

That's perspective right there, folks.

⌘

I LOOKED AT JANUARY 1 in Grandma's entries, looking for some kernel of truth. I found a lot of activities like I would on any other day—guests, weather forecast, cooking plans. Maybe that means January 1 is like any other day when you live as long as Grandma. I did find something interesting in 2009—mostly because Grandma mentions "popcorn balls" between comments about Jim's and Mary's health. It just seemed incongruous (but then, so is life):

Jan. 1, 2009: New Year's Day. Was up early to watch early news; had a lot of good entertainment. Jim stopped in p.m.; said he had the flu so didn't stay. Wally also stopped with two popcorn balls, and Mary called. She has the shingles. Was windy and blowing snow.

⌘

ONE WAY TO LIVE through 100 Minnesota winters was to do as Grandma did: Be grateful for the weather when it's good and don't complain when it's bad. "Cold, cold and more cold," she wrote in a letter in January 2014. "The weather forecast is for more but I think that's for south Minnesota. I guess I shouldn't complain. I can stay inside."

One of the more memorable "bad" weather days in Minnesota is still referred to as the Halloween blizzard. It occurred on Oct. 31, 1991, which was an early snow by any standard.

Here's how Grandma remembered it:

> *Oct. 31, 1991:* I drove uptown for a haircut. Also, stopped at Dean's. Worked on my second Christmas tree skirt; finished it. When I got home from cards, I drove to the senior center for cards [she recycled old greeting cards into new ones]. It had snowed while we were there. I had about 35-40 kids for tricks & treats. The weather was OK then yet.

> *Nov. 1:* Was blowing and storming this morning. I baked two batches of cookies (I serve at church on Sunday). Clarine, Dorothy, Freda and I rode with Victor to Pierson to play cards. My driveway was pretty well filled when I came home.

> *Nov. 2:* Had a big drift in front of the garage. Dorothy picked us all up for coffee. It was cold and windy. I did some reading and some sewing.

⌘

HOPE WAS ONE OF the ways she coped with winter: hope for spring. "What a day outside! Sounds like snow for every day," she wrote in a letter to me in 2013. "I, too, love spring when everything comes alive. So many shades of pretty green. Most people like fall and colored leaves, but not me. That means death. But spring is so slow coming. Did have a few days the robins are here. I feel so sorry for them."

"We haven't had any snow the last month but the air is still cool so I haven't done any raking yet," she wrote in a different letter to me in the early '90s when I was living in southern Ohio. "I'm sure you have spring weather there. Send some over our way."

Another year, April was more kind. In a letter to me in April 2000, she wrote, "It's wonderful to feel like it's really spring with the nice warm weather again."

FIFTEEN

Marking time

"I HAVE PEOPLE ASK me why I think I'm living so long," Grandma once told an interviewer about her longevity. "I don't have an answer, but I think there is a reason. There is something I have to do yet. I am getting forgetful. Maybe someday I will forget to wake up. I don't know, but I think I have something left to do. I had a good life and a good husband and kids. All of my life was good."

It doesn't take ten decades to get forgetful. Browsing my Facebook Newsfeed on the morning of March 8, 2014, I was astounded to see my cousin Paula wishing my grandmother happy birthday.

"Darn!" I thought (keeping it clean here—this book is G rated).

Grandma had turned 99. While I escaped winter and was enjoying the sunshine and spring training baseball in Fort Myers, Florida, my father's mother added another notch in the years-on-the-planet belt. How did it get to be March 8 so fast?! (Time marches quickly when the skies are clear, and the temps are in the 70s.)

Cousin Paula, with whom I was competing for Second Favorite Granddaughter honors, had posted the news. She was more on top of things than I was. Neither of us will ever claim the title of Most Favorite Granddaughter; that one belonged to Cousin Cheri, who was first grandchild overall and lived within ten minutes of Grandma's apartment. I added accolades every time I sent a letter from some far-flung location; Grandma loved mail. But Paula was the Only Daughter's Only Daughter, at that point, she had delivered two great-grandchildren and she was percolating a third, so we were in a close (ha!) race for Second Favorite (get in line, Kay, Betsy and Mollie).

Grandma didn't have favorites. I'm only kidding. This was a race only in my mind.

Within seconds of my announcement that I'd missed sending a card to Grandma for her birthday, my intrepid husband Tyler was on Google finding the florist nearest her. He called and asked if he could have flowers delivered today to a woman in town who was turning 99.

I swear. That was all he said. No name. No address. He provided his credit card and contact info, and a beautiful bouquet was on its way with an enclosure that said "Love, Monica."

I rocked.

Or at least my husband rocked. To-may-to, to-mah-to. The point is, Grandma lived in a town smallest enough to be the only resident turning 99 that day. Or she was that awesome.

She was that awesome.

Just-in-time delivery.

⌘

THERE'S A SAYING I like: "Even the moon passes through phases to return to full." It's a more lyrical reminder than "the only constant is change," that even when the moon is barely visible in the night sky and seems so far away, it will change again. When it seems it is about to disappear altogether, the moon will return to full.

One cannot page through twenty-five years Grandma's journals without being reminded everything comes back around. She planted in spring, she tended in summer, she harvested in autumn, and she rested in winter. She enjoyed strawberry pie in July and apple cake in November. She celebrated a special person's birthday year after year after year, and then when they were gone, she observed the anniversary of their death. She did the same things over and over again. She canned peaches, she did laundry, she walked daily, she went to church every Sunday.

Some might find Grandma's commitment to a schedule to be boring or rote, but she didn't. She turned dates into parties, everyday acts into lifetime habits, chores into traditions. She treasured the good things and endured the sorrows because she knew they wouldn't last forever.

The very last diary entry of Grandma's looked like it was written Saturday, Oct. 3, 2009. She was 94, and her handwriting was even more crooked and uneven than usual. Still, in the weeks running up to that entry, she noted she was making apple and pumpkin pies, doing laundry, writing letters, cooking apples and when my cousin Cheri's father-in-law died, she made a feast to give to Cheri when she had the kids home for the funeral: "two pumpkin pies, twenty chocolate cupcakes with cream filling and a cherry shortcake."

Saturday: *I was a little later but made the potato salad and got cake ready for dessert when Mary gets here. She got here at 9 so we had coffee and then went to Farmer's Market. Had very nice things. I bought a small squash and a zucchini. We also stopped at Wally and Jean's so had noon lunch a little later. Mary left at 3:30. Jim and Dianna walked down; they asked me to come for supper. Tim's and Cheri and Danny were there.*

And that's all she wrote. My father once mentioned Grandma went through some depression in her nineties, and maybe that's why she quit writing. When you can't say something positive, don't say anything at all.

⌘

GRANDMA'S COUSIN ALVINA SPENT Grandma's last birthday with her. Here is another contribution Alvina wrote for this book.

My Last Visit with Laura

It was her 104th birthday. My sister Jeannette and I decided to go together. As I planned our visit, I decided to make it very special. My sister had given me the "Bluebird Dishes" that had belonged to our grandmother. Laura's mother also had a set of those same dishes. I wondered if the sewing club that was started by those ladies was named after the dishes or if they got the dishes after naming the club the Bluebird Sewing Club. Laura was just a girl, along with her sisters Freda and Emelia. My mother was also a part of that club. As a child, I could remember playing under the quilt when the ladies came over to quilt or we went to their houses.

I knew using these dishes would be a special treat for Laura. We had Jell-O salad with fruit and whipped topping, kiwi and orange slices, sweet bread, cheese slices and cheesecake. I poured the coffee into the cup and set the table with a beautiful tablecloth. Once I put the dishes on the table, Laura marveled immediately by saying "Bluebird dishes". Even if her eyes were poor, she could tell what they were. The nurse had told us she hadn't eaten much before we came for her dinner, but she ate every bit of what I brought. I was so tickled to spend this time with her and make it special.

Once we were done, Jeannette cleared the dishes away and rinsed them off. Laura told me, "Gee, you really got her trained good." I just laughed. She always had something humorous to say.

Another joy that I had was that I could send pictures to her daughter Mary who was not able to come to Laura's birthday because of plans she and her husband had made for a trip. Sending those photos to her just blessed her to know her mom was having a really good birthday.

I know that Laura was looking forward to going to heaven and she was ready. Reality seemed to be elusive at times. I was okay with that. I know that she has been restored and is with those who put their trust in Jesus. They are all together celebrating in peace and joy.

I will never forget what Laura has meant to me through the years, but I am happy she is now at peace.

SIXTEEN

The funeral

GRANDMA WAS A TINY person physically, but she loomed large in her family in part because of her longevity. I have clear, vivid memories of her because I knew her when I was an adult, a *middle-aged* adult. We were pen pals for decades, and as the proud recipient of many of her diaries, I have relived many of her days with her as I paged through her journals.

I and so many others were the beneficiaries of her graceful hospitality. She was an incredible hostess, and I think of her whenever I use her china or enjoy a pickled beet. I also inherited her vanity, but I do not consider it a deadly sin. I believe part of the reason she lasted as long as she did is because she took care of her human vessel. She cared about how she looked, and an interest in fashion was part of that interest. She accented her outfits by wearing bracelets and scarves right up 'til the very end.

Grandma had a great sense of humor, and one of her favorite holidays was April Fools'

Day. She was also an avid gardener, which is no mean feat in north central Minnesota where the growing season is eight weeks long (I kid, but not much).

I cannot think of Grandma without thinking of hearing aids. I think losing her hearing was a difficult thing for someone as social as she was. It happened relatively early in her life; I don't even remember my grandmother without hearing aids. In the end she was so profoundly deaf, it was easier to get your point across with a white board than to yell. Her eyesight was failing, too, and in later years she began using a wheelchair more than her own legs. Aging is not for the faint-hearted, quite literally.

Before Grandma died, she planned her funeral, writing down many details so we would get it right. (Among the details she did not dictate, we draped one of her handmade quilts over her coffin instead of a spray of flowers; she was an avid quilter for many years, and it was beautiful. And her family, not Grandma, selected the wild rice hotdish for the funeral luncheon, but I found that a perfect choice for a Central Minnesota funeral.) For some reason, Grandma designated me to read one of the Bible readings at the service. Apparently, I had brought my public speaking skills to her attention in more than one postal missive I sent to her. Unlike some of my cousins who probably would not have wanted the burden, I was flattered to do it. When I looked up the verses before the service, I thought they was perfect for Grandma.

For to me to live is Christ, and to die is gain. If I am to live in the flesh, that means fruitful labor for me. Yet which I shall choose I cannot tell. I am hard pressed between the two. My desire is to depart and be with Christ, for that is far better. But to remain in the flesh is more necessary on your account.

~ Philippians 1:21-24

Grandma lived so long she came to wonder whether God had forgotten her or flat out didn't want her. The pastor at her funeral said her most persistent question was "Why am I still here?" The tone he parroted made her sound like she was cross examining him in a court of law.

Her reason for being is probably as varied as the people who knew her. For me, she was a role model for aging gracefully, if not always cheerfully. It's hard to get old, but she persevered because she believed in a higher purpose. And reading her journals, it is clear her gratitude got her through more than one unhappy occasion. The week her beloved sister Freda died, she remarked three times about the beautiful weather. She found something be thankful for even when sorrow could have overwhelmed her.

Fortunately for all of us and her, too, Grandma died in her sleep. God wanted her after all, He just didn't want her going out in a blaze of IV tubes and pain meds, so He waited out that strong heart of hers.

I was not sad Grandma died. She lived a good life, and she died a good death. I miss her, to be sure, and know many others miss here, too, but leaving this earthly plain is what she wanted so I was happy for her. Her send-off was oddly celebratory for a funeral, but perfectly pitched for someone who lived 104 years in God's grace.

Two hundred and eight people attended Grandma's funeral, which is a lot when you think about how old she was and how many of her friends died before she did. Grandma was buried in Haycreek Cemetery, near her husband and her sister, six and half miles from where she was born.

So, how do you live to be 104?

Faith, family, frugality, fun and fresh fruits and vegetables.

At least that's how Grandma did it.

Acknowledgements

BY THE TIME THIS book comes out, Grandma Laura will have been gone nearly two years. It doesn't seem that long, but then a pandemic year also makes it seem like an eternity. This book would not have been possible if Grandma didn't have the wherewithal to keep up with her diaries and the foresight to gift them to me. Thank you, Grandma, for role modeling how to age gracefully. May heaven be all you hoped it would be.

My deepest and most heartfelt thanks go to people who knew Grandma better than I did: my dad, Aunt Mary, Aunt Jean and Cousin Cheri shared many memories of her with me, and this book would be less complete without them. Thank you for your patience as I pulled this book together.

Though we have not met, Alvina Kytta was very generous in contributing stories of Grandma for this book. It is clear from Grandma's diaries that Grandma treasured their visits.

Kudos to my cousin Paula who agreed to take multiple photos of Grandma's quilts so I could create a book cover that speaks to Grandma's talents.

To my mother for all her help, guidance, editing and photos. She is a fine sounding board who tolerates my procrastination with patience.

And to my readers, whether you are related to me or not, thank you for your continued interest in my writing. Your attention gives me faith in my craft.

About the Author

MONICA LEE IS THE author of several memoirs, including *The Percussionist's Wife: A Memoir of Sex, Crime & Betrayal*, about her first marriage and *Church Sweet Home: A Renovation to Warm the Soul*, an adventure in home renovation with her second husband. She is a personal historian, blogger and writer who helps her husband make money by filling out boring insurance paperwork, but her real love is writing. Follow news about her writing at http://mindfulmonica.wordpress.com or catch up with her everyday life on her blog at http://minnesotatransplant.wordpress.com.

Made in the USA
Las Vegas, NV
14 January 2021

15925044R00083